Fig. 3re

Fig. 4

CLOCKS & WATCHES

CLOCKS & WATCHES

Eric Bruton

PAUL HAMLYN

London New York Sydney Toronto

Published by
THE HAMLYN PUBLISHING GROUP LIMITED
Hamlyn House · Feltham · Middlesex · England
© *Copyright The Hamlyn Publishing Group Limited 1968*
Second impression 1969
Printed in Italy by Arnoldo Mondadori Editore · Verona
SBN 6000 0642 5

Frontispiece
Elaborate enamelled and gem-set automaton clock
which was a present from King George III of England to the
Emperor Kien-Lung of China about 1790.
It was made by Henry Borell of London. At the hour a little
door opens below the dial and ships are seen moving
on simulated waves. The height is thirty-five inches
JÜRG STUKER GALLERY, BERNE, SWITZERLAND

Contents

The double-twelve astronomical dial of Wells Cathedral clock. The original clock of 1392 had no dial and this was added a century or more later. It shows hours, days, dates, and moon phases. Above are four mounted knights who joust. The Wells clock is unique in the world because it chimes and strikes simultaneously in two different places inside and outside the cathedral. The clock operates the oldest automaton, Jack Blandifer

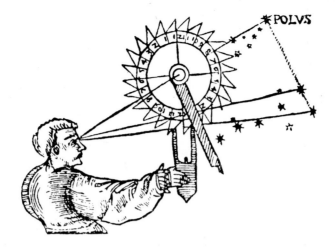

Author's preface

Most people take the accuracy of their clocks and watches and of the time service for granted. Yet it has taken over six thousand years to reach today's standards.

For a long period religious sects were those most preoccupied with timekeeping. The monks of the Dark Ages chanted verses to mark the canonical hours. After mechanical timekeepers came on the scene – clocks about A D 1300 and watches around 1500 – they became the status symbols of the time, like fast cars and yachts today.

The fact that 16th-century watch and clockmakers were as valuable to their communities as 20th-century atomic scientists to theirs has long been forgotten, as has the fact that clocks and watches were the first technical products to open up Europe's trade with the East. In the 18th and early 19th centuries it was the mastery of timekeeping at sea, hence accurate navigation, that led to the domination of the British Navy, the acquisition of the British Empire, and accurate charting of the world's coastlines.

Many essentials of modern life were first the brainchildren of clock and watchmakers – the chain drive, for example, and the cardan shaft and differential gearing used in the back axles of motor cars, the thermostat in every oven, and the principle of feedback in automation. Today space travel would be impossible without quartz clocks and the atomic clock that is accurate to the equivalent of one second in three thousand years.

There are several people whose help in the preparation of the book I want to acknowledge; most of all

that of Mr. Philip Coole, of the British Museum, with his valuable comments and suggestions, and the Museum itself for the exceptionally fine facilities provided by the Ilbert Students' Room. I appreciate particularly the opportunity provided for me to take those colour pictures in the book that do not carry a credit line. All the items are from the British Museum's collection.

My appreciative thanks are due to Mr. Orville Hagans, of the Hagans Clock Manor Museum, Manor Heights, Bergen Park, Evergreen, Colorado, and to Mr. J. E. Coleman for considerable help with pictures, and with checking the chapter on American horological history. Mr. Hagans' museum is a remarkable private venture to spread the knowledge of horology. Another American, Mr. Charles Terwilliger, of Bronxville, New York, very kindly provided me with colour pictures of some items in his unique collection of Bilston boxes imitating watches.

For much of the information about John Harrison, I am indebted to Colonel H. Quill, past Master of the Worshipful Company of Clockmakers, who has written a biography of that extraordinary clockmaker.

A number of the drawings in the illustration by Mr. A. E. Ayres on page 32 were based on a selection of the three thousand in De Carle's 'Clock and Watch Encyclopedia' and I am obliged to the publishers, N.A.G. Press Ltd., London, for permission to use them in this way.   ERIC BRUTON

ABOVE: Drawing from Apians Cosmographicus Liber *of 1533, showing how a nocturnal is used to tell the time at night from the Great Bear*

The first timekeepers

Man's first clock was himself.

Every living organism has a built-in 'biological clock' that controls its habits. Many of man's psychological activities, such as the times at which he feels hungry, are geared to twenty-four-hour rhythm. It is often quite difficult to reset this system, to adapt it to a new time routine. There are also lunar-daily, monthly, and yearly cycles.

Experiments with cockroaches have shown that they have a master clock system that controls their activities in relation to day and night. The master clock has dominance over a subsidiary clock which prevents the general pattern of behaviour from being upset during short periods of darkness during daylight, as when the insect crawls under a stone.

The behaviour of plants as well as animals has been studied and related to these cycles. The growth of a potato, for example, has a daily cycle related to the lunar month.

An awareness that the human being incorporated a kind of clock mechanism existed at an early date. Plautus, the Roman poet who died about 184 B C, wrote:

> *The gods confound the man who first found out*
> *How to distinguish hours. Confound him, too,*
> *Who in this place set up a sundial,*
> *To rub and hack my days so wretchedly*
> *Into small pieces! When I was a boy*
> *My belly was my sundial – one more sure,*
> *Truer, and more exact than any one of them.*

The measurement of time by an instrument is one of man's earliest scientific achievements. The first time interval of which he became aware was undoubtedly the day, marked by the rising and setting sun. Then, perhaps, in the early civilizations around the Mediterranean shores, he noted that the flooding of the Nile marked a lengthier interval on which the growing of food depended. He would have become aware of the cycle of the moon every month, since he had to rely on its light at night, and of the rise and fall of the tides when he sailed or fished.

Nature provides a number of natural clocks. The passage of the sun (or, as it was later discovered, the rotation of the Earth) marks the interval known as a day. Repetition of the moon's phases marks a month. The recurring seasons indicate the lapse of a year. The week is a man-made invention. So is the hour, a very early division of time.

At some point in civilisation, the need arose for the division of daylight into parts. It is most likely that this happened among the people of the Near East – the Egyptians, Chaldeans, Assyrians, Phoenicians, and the Hebrews, Medes, and Persians – who lived in the delta of the Nile, Euphrates, and Tigris, and the basin of the Indus.

Around 4000 B C, villagers used the shadow of a tall palm tree as it moved across the ground to indicate the intervals of daylight. Palm trees die eventually. They bend in the wind, too, and might not be conveniently placed for more urban civilisations. At some period, a person in authority thought of replacing the palm by a tall stone or obelisk to indicate the hour by its shadow.

One of the most famous of these was the Obelisk of Luxor, the ancient city of Thebes. It now stands in the centre of the Place de la Concorde in Paris. Rome has about twenty obelisks in various squares, carried there by early Emperors, and in London, on the Thames Embankment, is the famous Cleopatra's Needle, sister of a similar column near Cairo. Cleopatra's Needle was first erected at Heliopolis about 1500 B C, and removed to Alexandria by order of Caesar Augustus in 23 B C. It was brought to London at the beginning of the last century.

Days were divided into hours, but not the hours we use today. Early civilisations regarded days and nights as quite separate periods, and divided each into the same number of 'temporal hours', usually twelve. Only the astronomers lumped day and night together as one period, dividing it into twenty-four hours of equal lengths. These 'equal hours' did not come into use in civil life until the 14th century A D. A relic of the fact that day and night were regarded as separate times remains in the English language, which has no exact word for a period of day and night.

The length of a temporal hour of the day was therefore different from a temporal hour of the night, and both varied in length according to the season of the year except at the equinoxes, when they were equal. In the early civilisations of the Mediterranean, the variation was small because at all times of the years day-time and night-time do not vary much in length. In northern Europe, however, nights in winter could be more than twice as long as those in summer, so the hours were also more than twice as long.

To start daylight hours from dawn introduced the difficulty of deciding exactly when dawn began. Some thousands of years later the Muslims decreed that it should start when it was possible to distinguish black threads from white ones in a tassel.

About 4000 B C, the Egyptians employed twelve temporal hours and divided the month into three 'decades' of ten days each, probably because they counted on their fingers. The French revolutionaries tried to replace the twelve hours of the day and twelve months of the year by ten, nearly six thousand years later.

TOP LEFT: A Roman hemicycle sundial, designed by the Chaldean astronomer Berosus about 290 BC. The spike which forms the style is missing SCIENCE MUSEUM, LONDON

RIGHT: Cleopatra's Needle, now on the Thames Embankment, London, was probably the style of a huge sundial after it was erected on the Heliopolis by Pharaoh Thothmes III about 1500 BC. The inscriptions were added about two hundred years later by Ramses the Great

Why the day became divided into twelve hours is not known, but it is possibly associated with the magical significance of that number. There were twelve Great Gods of Olympus, twelve Labours of Hercules, twelve Tables of Roman Law, and twelve Apostles of Jesus Christ.

As well as public shadow clocks, there were portable ones for business or domestic use. The earliest surviving shadow clock is portable, a fragment from Egypt dated about 1500 BC, now in the Berlin Museum. It is T-shaped and arranged so that a shadow of the crosspiece falls on the main stem, which is marked in hours.

A large Egyptian sundial found in excavations is in the form of a flight of steps on which the shadow of a wall falls. The first authentic reference known to a sundial – in the Bible, Second Book of Kings, Chapter twenty – is to one of this type which belonged to King Ahaz. On it, Isaiah the Prophet performed the miracle of moving the shadow of the sun backwards by four degrees. The revised edition of the Bible uses the word 'steps' instead of 'degrees'. The date was about 695 BC.

Egyptian astronomers knew how to find the time at night by observing the passage of certain stars as they came into line with two plumb lines on successive nights, but this technique was too scientific for households, which used water clocks at night and in cloudy weather. An early Egyptian hieroglyph is believed to be of a water clock.

A water clock, also called a clepsydra (Greek: stealer of water), operated by water dripping from a small hole near the bottom of a vessel, and slowly filling another vessel. The walls of one of the two were marked to indicate the hours. There is a record of a water clock with a drilled gemstone for the hole, to reduce wear – the first jewelled timepiece!

A clepsydra reconstructed from pieces found in the Egyptian Temple of Karnak and dated about 1400 BC shows that some sophistication was needed to design even these elementary water clocks. The stone sides are sloped so that the level of water falls uniformly although the water runs out less rapidly as the level falls.

Sand glasses came later than water clocks. They were constructed on the same principle as clepsydras, measuring the passage of time by sand running from a container into a lower one, which was sometimes marked with a scale. Egypt, of course, was not short of sand and in its hot dry climate the mobility of sand was obvious.

The sand glass has had an extremely long life and is still common today as an egg-timer. Ships of the Royal Navy had four-hour sand glasses to time watches until as late as 1839 and the Speaker of the House of Commons used a two-minute sand glass to time divisions until after the Second World War, but that of course was for traditional reasons. In 16th-century England the 'sermon glass' or 'pulpit hour glass' was common in churches

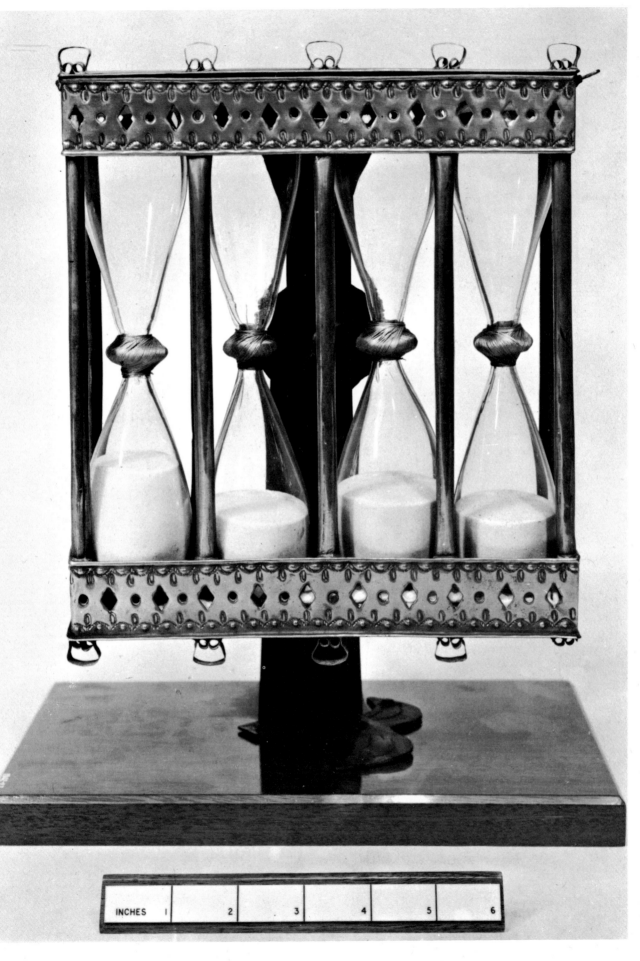

INCHES 1 2 3 4 5 6

Cast of an Egyptian water clock of 1415 to 1380 BC from Karnak Temple. Water ran out from a hole on the right. Scales showing the time are inside SCIENCE MUSEUM, LONDON

for preachers to time their sermons. Domestic sand glasses sometimes contained several sets of glasses giving intervals of quarter, half, three-quarters, and one hour. The 'sand' was often powdered egg shell.

Egyptian sundials and water clocks were introduced into Greece and used extensively during the times of the Greek and Roman Empires. Their accuracy was

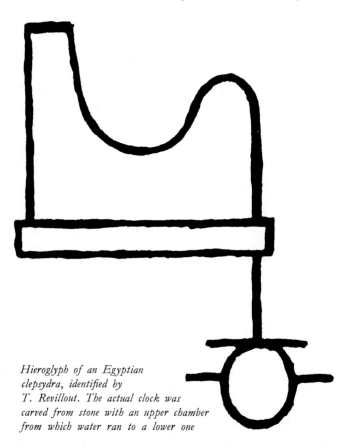

Hieroglyph of an Egyptian clepsydra, identified by T. Revillout. The actual clock was carved from stone with an upper chamber from which water ran to a lower one

improved by inscribing them with different scales for different times of the year to suit the different lengths of temporal hours. One type of sundial was the hemispherium, a hemispherical hollow in the top of a block of stone. An upright spike from the centre of the bottom was the style which threw a shadow on the scales engraved round the inside of the hollow.

As nearly half the hemispherium was inoperative at night, the Chaldean astronomer Berosus modified it in about 290 B C, cutting away the useless half. This type, the 'hemicycle', came into common use.

About 150 B C, Hipparchus, the Greek, invented an elaborate kind of altitude dial for finding the time in either temporal or equal hours. It is a disc with moveable sighting bar on one side to measure the sun's altitude. On the other side is a star map. It is called an 'astrolabe' and was simplified by Martin Behaim of Nuremberg many centuries later, in about 1480, to become the mariners' astrolabe for ships' navigators.

Considerable efforts were made by the mechanician over two thousand years ago to improve timekeepers, particularly the water clock or clepsydra. After Alexandria became the metropolis of the civilised world, Ctesibius, who worked in the School of Alexandria, invented a large and elaborate clepsydra, about 300 years B C. It was based on the principles of hydraulics discovered some years earlier by Archimedes. The cylindrical dial was marked with hours and rotated. The time was indicated by a stationary statue holding a lance.

The clock was a master work of its time and was copied in other places. Vitruvius, a Roman architect who lived in the Ist century B C, designed a very similar large clock but employed a rotating hand on a twentyfour-hour dial marked from I to XII and then from I to XII again. This is known as a 'double twelve dial'. It also had a rotating dial which indicated the sign of the zodiac and other information against a fixed hand. It was driven like the water clock of Ctesibius, by a rope wound round a barrel which turned gear wheels. One end of the rope carried a small weight and the other end was attached to a float which rose with the level of water in a tank. The rate of water flowing into the tank was carefully regulated.

Writing about 30 B C, Vitruvius described how the water flow was kept constant although the head of water changed, and how the scales of hours had to be varied to suit the temporal hours at different times of the year. He also detailed thirteen different types of sundial.

Unscrupulous Roman lawyers whose speeches were timed by water clock used to gain time, it is said, by secretly dropping a little mud into the water to slow down the clock.

Water clocks became more and more ingenious and complicated in the first few centuries of the Christian era, although the most elaborate were not made in the

Christian world. The Emperor Charlemagne received a lepsydra in the 9th century A D from Haroun-al-Rachid, the potentate of Baghdad. It was made of bronze inlaid with gold. Gifford reports in his 'History of France' that the dial was composed of twelve small doors, which represented the hours. 'Each door opened at the hour it was intended to represent and out of it came the same number of little balls, which fell one by one on a brass drum. When it was twelve o'clock, twelve horsemen in miniature issued forth at the same time and shut all the doors.'

In A D 725, a Buddhist monk and military official, I'Hsing, devised what is today called an 'escapement' for a water clock. The function of any escapement is to control the rate at which the clock goes. The Chinese replaced the dripping water, rising float, and lowered weight of the earlier water clocks, by a water wheel. The wheel was turned by a flow of water like the wheel of a water mill, but the rate at which it turned was controlled by a clever system of weighbridges. A working model can be seen in the Science Museum, London.

In 1090, a Chinese statesman and scientist called Su Sung wrote about an amazing astronomical water clock he had made. Su Sung's clock incorporated I'Hsing's escapement and was probably the finest medieval Chinese clock. It stood almost forty feet high. The huge water wheel and other mechanism were installed in the base and on one side was a pagoda with tiers of puppets which paraded to show and sound the hours and quarters. The upper storey contained a celestial sphere rotated by the clock. On the top was a railed platform, reached by outside steps, where an armillary sphere (model of the Universe made of metal rings) was automatically pointed by the clock at certain stars, like a modern observatory telescope.

Fire clocks were used almost as extensively as water clocks from about the 9th century A D in the Far East. The earliest was probably the match cord which burned like a fuse and was knotted at intervals to indicate hours. The Chinese employed a double twelve-hour system, probably introduced from Babylonia.

The most common form of fire clock was the joss stick clock or incense clock. The joss stick, a mixture of clay and the sawdust of aromatic woods with some musk and gold dust pasted with water and glue on a long, thin sliver of bamboo, was marked at intervals representing the hours as it burned down. Some were made to burn for several days. Miners in some parts of China today are said still to use incense stick clocks that smoulder for three hours.

Most elaborate of the fire clocks was the incense seal, a flat piece of stone or metal with a channel in the surface marked off in hours in which powdered incense was placed and lit at one end. Some had simple up and down tracks; in others the track was circular; and some had channels formed like a maze. The hours were sometimes indicated by small pegs of bamboo. Once the powder had been lit, it continued burning along the channel at an even rate without a flame. Some incense seals had perforated covers to protect them from draughts.

Incense seals were made in China until modern times. Seen in curio shops, they are hardly ever recognised as fire clocks and usually identified as opium stoves, hand warmers or something else.

The Chinese even had a fire alarm, called the 'dragon boat'. There is one in the Musée de la Marine, at the Louvre in Paris. An incense stick rests on wires along the length of the 'boat' and is lit at one end. Across the place corresponding to the time required, a length of thread with a weight each end is hung. When the burning end of the incense stick reaches the place just under the thread, the thread burns and the little weights drop into a metal dish with a clang.

Chinese fire clocks were introduced into Japan between the 6th and 9th centuries, the joss clocks being known as 'Chinese matches'. A special type of joss stick interval timer for geisha houses became popular from as late as the 17th century until recent times to calculate

Water clock at Bou Inaria in Fez, ancient capital of the Moorish Empire. The thirteen brass gongs seen on the wall on the left, were struck by hammers from the doors above

ABOVE: *Japanese geisha timepiece, like an eight and a half long wooden match box, holding joss sticks. As a joss stick is lit to indicate a time interval, it is stood in a hole in the top* MR. SILVIO BEDINI, NEW YORK, USA

RIGHT: *A Chinese fire clock with its lid on to avoid effects of draughts. Under the lid is a channel, like a maze, along which powder slowly burns* THE SMITHSONIAN INSTITUTION, USA

BELOW: *Chinese dragon vessel of lacquered wood used as an alarm clock. A description of the action appears on page 17* WUPPERTALER UHRENMUSEUM, W. GERMANY

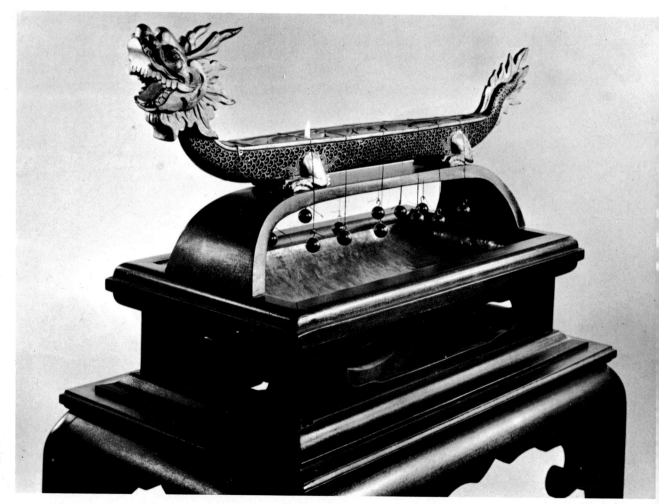

charges for entertainment. The joss sticks were kept in a special box. One type of box had a sloping front like an old school desk. Along the top was a row of holders for the joss sticks with a peg in front of each on which was hung an ivory tablet bearing the name of the girl concerned. As a girl retired with a guest, a joss stick was lit and placed above her name.

A 'flower girl' might earn several sticks during a day, and even now in Japan, although joss sticks are no longer seen, it is customary to ask 'What is the price of a flower girl incense stick?'

Japanese incense seals were made in the form of hardwood boxes, somewhat larger than the Chinese metal ones, and lacquered in clear red or black or a combination of these colours.

The Saxons, the Teutonic race that had conquered England by the 7th century, used marked candles for telling the time. Asser, the biographer of King Arthur, tells of the king using candles to divide his working day. Each candle burned for four hours. It was used in a lantern made of wood with windows of thin, almost transparent horn.

It is also possible that the Saxons were among the first to use lamp clocks. The oil for the lamp was contained in a reservoir and the amount of oil left showed the amount of time elapsed. Some much later versions had glass reservoirs. Lamp clocks were in common use until the 19th century for telling the time at night.

A particularly elementary water clock was used by the Saxons as a timer. Known as 'sinking bowls', those surviving are nothing more than bronze bowls six inches or more in diameter, each with a hole in the bottom. Placed on the surface of still water, the bowl sinks in a given time. The lengths of time for which irrigation channels are opened to different farmers' fields are still timed in this way in Algeria.

The Saxons did not employ hours, but divided the day into four roughly equal 'tides,' a word that has survived in our expressions 'noontide' and 'eventide'. Their sundials, of which several are still in existance, were marked in tides. One of the best examples is on Bewcastle Cross, in Cumberland, and has been dated about A D 670. Another was marked on Kirkdale Church, Yorkshire, about A D 1060.

Cruder shadow clocks can be found on many old churches which date from the 12th to the 15th centuries. They were usually scratched on one of the vertical stones of the south porch and look very much like the broad arrow now denoting government property. Some churches have several. 'Scratch dials' were probably made by the priest to show the times of services. Consequently they vary considerably in the spacing and number of lines. They are often called 'Mass dials' because they indicated the times of Mass. A few scratch dials made after about 1500 are quite sophisticated and, like that on Litlington Church, in Sussex, show hours of equal length.

The Egyptian T-shaped shadow clock of the 10th to 8th century B C, referred to earlier, was portable, but most early sundials were permanent. The T-shaped shadow clock was what is now called an 'altitude dial' because its operation depends on the height the sun reaches in the sky. It is noon when the sun is at its meridian, its highest point, and the shadow is at its shortest. As long as the shadow clock is placed on a relatively flat surface and the T-bar is towards east in the morning and west after noon, it will record the temporal hour.

Another type of portable sundial depends on the direction of the sun as it appears to move from east to west, and is called a 'compass dial'. The sundial has to be set up so that the style or gnomon is in a north-south direction. Almost all garden sundials are of this type.

Permanent sundials from earliest times were of both types, but *portable* ones were all altitude dials until the compass was invented and it was possible to orientate a portable sundial at a few moments' notice by finding north by compass and turning the portable sundial to point in the correct direction before reading the shadow.

Reconstruction of the astronomical water clock built by Su Sung c. 1090. This model is in the Chinese Peoples Republic

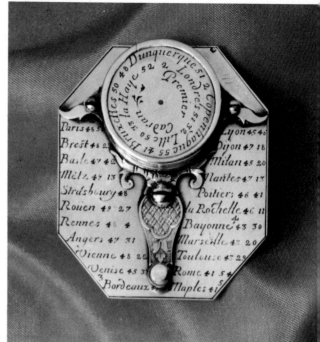

ABOVE: Front and back of a silver compass dial of c. 1700 *signed Butterfield of Paris, and shown actual size. The angle of the gnomon can be altered according to different places. The place names and angle (latitudes) are engraved on the back* ASPREYS OF BOND STREET, LONDON

LEFT: A 14th-century brass astrolabe, three and a half inches in diameter, for telling the time by the sun's altitude. This side (the 'rete') shows a star map CAIUS COLLEGE, CAMBRIDGE

RIGHT: A nocturnal of c. 1500 *made of wood covered with painted paper* GERMANISCHES NATIONALMUSEUM, NUREMBERG

BELOW: Water clocks like these were made about fifty years ago, not in the 17th century as often believed. This is a page from the catalogue of the makers, Pearson-Page of Birmingham, published about 1920

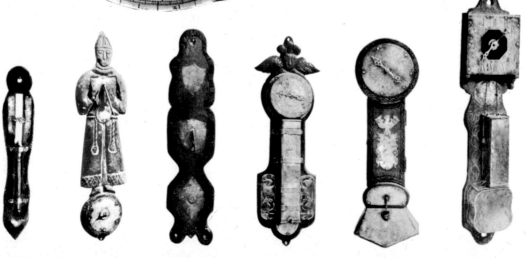

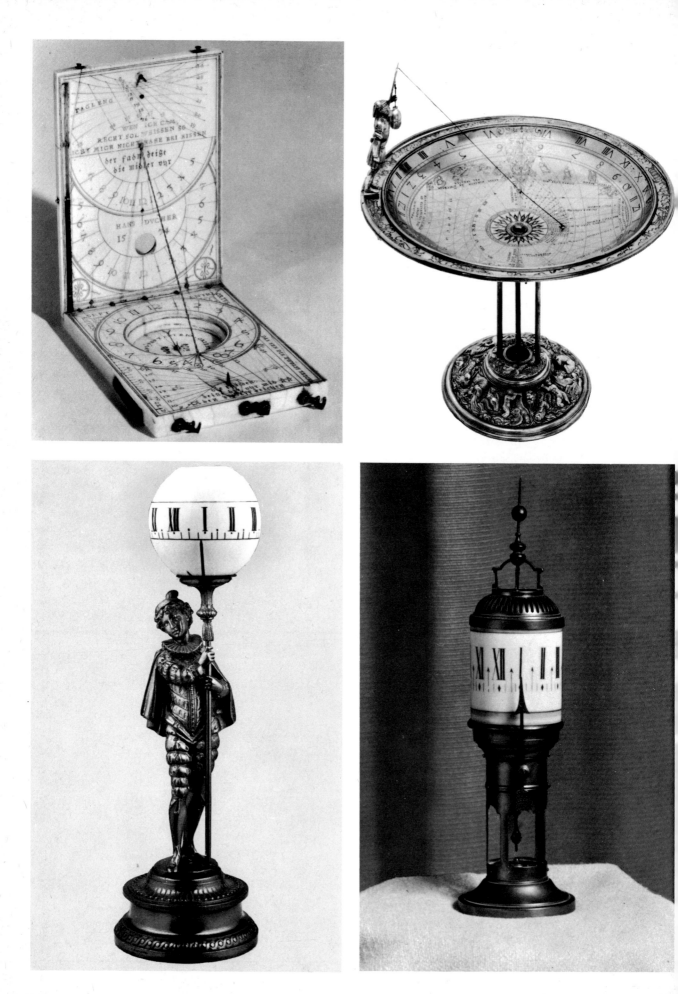

As the compass was not introduced into Europe until the 12th century, earlier portable dials are all altitude dials.

A portable sundial of Roman times was most likely to be a small cylinder hung from a thread. The shadow of a horizontal peg near the top fell along the length of the cylinder and an incised scale indicated the hour by the length of the shadow, i.e. the sun's altitude. There were different scales for different months of the year. Cylinder sundials like this have been used until recent times in the Pyrenees districts between France and Spain. They are known as 'shepherd's dials'.

In 1938, a 10th-century Saxon portable dial of the same type, but tablet-shaped and marked in tides, was found in the earth of the Cloister Garth at Canterbury Cathedral. It is made of silver with a gold pin, which has a gem-set animal's head for the gnomon. The pin fits in a hole in the bottom when not in use.

About 1400, another kind of portable altitude dial was invented and came into wide use in the following years. It looks like a napkin ring and is also held suspended from a thread in the hand. The sun's rays pass through a small hole in the side and the spot of light on the inner opposite side indicates the time on a scale of hours.

A compass dial had a built-in compass and was turned so that the needle pointed north-south. The gnomon was often a thread. Many compass dials were produced in the 16th and 17th centuries for carrying in a pocket. They were of brass or wood and the better ones were of ivory or silver. Many were formed of two tablets hinged at one end like a book, and are called 'tablet sundials'. Often they are beautifully engraved and decorated and works of art in their own right. One tablet, thicker than the other, carries the compass, sunk in it, with the sundial engraved around it. When the other tablet, which forms the lid, is hinged open until it is upright, a cord is stretched between the two, to form the gnomon and cast a shadow on the scale.

In all early sundials, the gnomon was a rod or post placed vertically, horizontally, or at some arbitrary angle to cast the shadow showing the time. The scales on these sundials were suitable only for the latitude in which they were marked. The Arab astronomers discovered that if the gnomon were placed parallel to the earth's axis, the sundial would read the same at any latitude. Pocket compass dials made in the 18th century sometimes had a hinged gnomon, the angle of which could be altered according to figures engraved on the back, so that compass dials could be used in places of different latitudes.

About 1520, astronomers noted that the star constellations moved round the Pole Star in twenty-four sidereal hours. They invented an instrument called a 'nocturnal' for telling the time by the stars at night. It is adjusted for the date, held upright by its handle and the Pole Star sighted through a hole in the centre. A lever is then lined up with two stars of the Great Bear (Big Dipper) or Little Bear and gives the hour on a scale.

Well before then, however, the centres of learning had moved from the Near and Far East to Europe, and it was in Europe that the mechanical clock was born, some time before the year 1300.

A 17th-century column sundial with a rotatable dragon on top whose tail acts as the style. The dragon's tail is turned until it is over the appropriate month, shown by signs of the zodiac at the bottom and the knob reached by the shadow of the tip shows the time SCIENCE MUSEUM, LONDON

23

Birth of the mechanical clock

After the Caesars' legions imposed the Roman way of life on Europe, there was a long period of stability and learning from the new masters, who introduced such sophisticated devices as baths, underfloor heating, and water clocks. It was also a time when the ideas of Christianity were spreading rapidly through Europe, largely through the teaching of the Celts.

The Roman Empire crumbled and was left in ruins by successive tides of murdering Goths and Huns. The terrible Dark Ages enveloped Europe and learning came to an end, except in the Celtic monasteries in remote places that survived the marauders. A monastery was a self-contained community which had its own fields, granaries, workshops, and living quarters, grouped round a central church. It was run on strictly ordered lines with times for working and times for praying and sleeping, but no time for idleness which Satan could exploit.

The very strict Benedictine Order, founded by St. Benedict of Nursia (A D c. 480-543) in a monastery on Monte Cassino in Italy, was ruled entirely by the clock. A bell ringer was responsible for sounding a large bell, that could be heard in the fields as well as in the buildings, to divide the day into 'canonical hours'. The word 'canon' means 'measuring rod' and canonical hours were the times for chanting prayers. The most usual method of gauging time was by chanting verses. Originally there were three canonical hours, which were increased to five, six, and then by St. Benedict, to seven. Two still survive in church services, matins and vespers.

The bell ringer consulted a sundial by day and the stars by night to decide the time. Cloudy weather complicated the bell ringer's task and Cassiodorus, a monk and Roman statesman who built a Benedictine monastery on his estate, reported, 'I have built for you a sun dial and a water clock... water serves as a miraculous substitute for the burning power of the sun in the heavens.' He was full of praise for timekeepers in monastic life, remarking that horologium – the word used for all kinds of timekeepers in early writings – were invented 'for the utmost benefit of the human race'. Another Benedictine monk, Hildemar, went further, declaring 'No prayer is rational unless timed by a clepsydra indicating the hours at night-time or on a grey day.'

Many monasteries had clepsydrae. There is a report that when the platform holding the shrine at the monastery of St. Edmundsbury in England caught fire, it was just as the horologium struck matins and 'our young men therefore ran for water, some to the well, some to the clock; others with great difficulty extinguished the violence of the fire with their cowls.' Not all monasteries could afford clepsydras or had the skill and knowledge to construct them, so the bell ringer or sacristan used a time candle. Even today the custom has survived in some places, with Easter candles banded to show the intervals for praying.

Among scholastic monks there were mechanicians and astronomers interested in timekeeper mechanisms. It was one of these, perhaps, who invented the mechanical clock during the Middle Ages, the period in Europe of rediscovery and development. From many references to horologium, or the derived names of horloge, or horloge in English, orologio in Italian, and reloge, orloge and other names in French, it has been impossible up to now to discover exactly where, when, and by whom it was invented.

Clepsydrae of the time were all mechanical except for the controlling part, the time standard, which was hydraulic – dripping water. The man who invented the mechanical clock replaced dripping water by a mechanical oscillator and connected this to the clock mechanism by what is called an 'escapement'. The birth of the mechanical clock may have been in France, Germany, or Italy; each has a claim. It occurred probably during the last quarter of the 12th century.

It is surmised that the first mechanical clocks were small alarms that alerted the sacristan to his duty of ringing the big bell, and that they were replacements for less reliable devices such as water clocks and time candles. Another theory is that the simple clock was part of a much more elaborate astronomical mechanism and was made separately because it was found to have a general use.

The word 'clock' seems to have come into use about 1330, when Richard of Wallingford used it to describe his amazing mechanical astronomical clock in notes for the monks, now in the Bodleian Library, Oxford. There are writings of 1371 referring to 'clok' and 'Tell itte be

TOP LEFT: An Italian monastic alarm of perhaps the 15th century, made of brass, as were early astrolabes. Such clocks were probably the prototypes of all alarms. Dante refers in 'Paradise Lost' (1312) to small clocks being well-known by everyone.
The clock was weight-driven and the alarm set by pins screwed in the holes round the double XII (twenty-four hour) dial.
The arm is a later addition. At the top is the balance wheel.

TOP RIGHT: The earliest night clock known made in the first half of the 15th century. It rings the bell at each 'hour'. The knobs are for finding the hour by touch. There are sixteen divisions round the dial
GERMANISCHES NATIONALMUSEUM, NUREMBERG

RIGHT: A south or mid-German Gothic wall clock of about 1380. It has capstan winding and a brass bell with a stone inside, like a cow bell. The small cranked handle at the bottom winds the alarm. Note the adjustable weights of the swinging foliot at the top. The driving weights are not original
MAINFRANKISCHES MUSEUM, WÜRZBURG

hegh none smytyn by ye clocke'. It is significant that the Middle English word is derived from the Latin *Clocca*, meaning 'bell'.

Most likely the first monastic alarm merely struck a single note on a bell and had no dial, but it may have had a simple rotating dial marked with hours and indicating against a fixed pointer.

It seems likely that domestic alarms were amongst the earliest clocks made. They were probably constructed of iron, although brass was being introduced at this time. Giovanni Dondi, professor of astronomy at Padua University, Italy, left a detailed description of a complex astronomical clock which he completed in 1364, in which he referred to 'common clocks'. A clock was made from Dondi's original instructions by Thwaites and Reed of London, under the guidance of Mr. H. Alan Lloyd in 1960 for the Smithsonian Institution in the USA.

Public clocks were being erected around 1300. The Signore – the city councils formed from the guilds of craftsmen in medieval Italy – anxious to free themselves from the domination of the church, began erecting bell towers all over the country to sound the curfew (when

citizens had to put out their fires), the tocsin (an emergency being declared), and other warnings. Many of these towers still exist in Italy, France, Germany, and Switzerland, although almost all now house relatively modern clocks.

Such a tower at first contained a bell that was rung by a bell ringer who was warned by a small alarm in the same way as the sacristan in the monastery. Tower warden's alarms – or 'belfry alarms' as they are also called – still exist. There is one in the Mainfrankische Museum, in Würzburg, that has been dated at about 1380. If the date is correct, it is the oldest clock still in existence.

Eventually the man with an alarm who rung a big bell was replaced by a large clock that could automatically sound a bell loudly enough to be heard in the surrounding country. A record of 1286 refers to a daily allowance of a loaf of bread to Bartholomo Orologiario, the clock keeper at old St. Paul's in London. In 1292 a 'new large clock' was installed at a cost of £ 30. At about the same time, in the courtyard of the old Palace of Westminster in London, was installed 'a Tower of Stone, containing

FAR LEFT: The outside dial at Wells Cathedral
MR. T. R. ROBINSON, BRISTOL

LEFT: The medieval astronomical dial at Wells Cathedral
MR. T. R. ROBINSON, BRISTOL

ABOVE: Modern jacks – the Smiths of Pelham Street, above an
ironmongers, Lewis & Grundy, Nottingham, which is worked
by a Cope clock MR. T. R. ROBINSON, BRISTOL

RIGHT: The blacksmith who strikes the bell at Abinger
Hammer in Surrey MR. T. R. ROBINSON, BRISTOL

Clock, which striketh every Hour on a great Bell...
for the same Clock in a Calm will be heard in the City
of London.'

Salisbury Cathedral clock is the oldest still going. It
was originally in a 13th-century bell tower in the Close
and was reinstalled in the cathedral in the 18th century.
At some time it was converted to pendulum operation, was
'lost', rediscovered (by T. R. Robinson in 1929), x-rayed
to discover which parts had been altered, restored to its
original condition in 1954, and now stands working in
the west nave of the cathedral. The clock is dated reli-

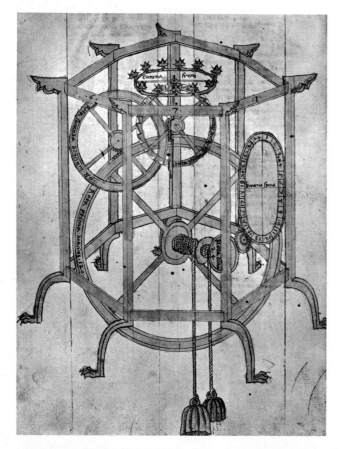

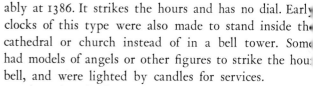

LEFT: *Dondi's own drawing of the frame and timekeeping part of his astronomical clock completed about 1364, in Padua, Italy*

BOTTOM LEFT: *Reproduction of Dondi's astronomical clock of c. 1364, which has some very complicated gearing. It was made in London in 1960 from the original instructions and is now in the Smithsonian Institution USA*

RIGHT: *Timekeeping train of the old clock at Salisbury showing the crown wheel and foliot, at the top, which is not original. Note how the frame is assembled with wedges in tenon slots at the top left. There are no nuts and bolts*

FAR RIGHT: *Astronomical dial of the 15th-century Exeter Cathedral clock. The Earth is the centre and round it revolves the moon in twenty-nine and a half days and the sun in twenty-four hours* MR. T. R. ROBINSON, BRISTOL

BOTTOM RIGHT: *An astronomical clock in Prague originally made at the end of the 15th century. It was badly damaged in the Second World War and restored, for the fourth time, in 1951*

ably at 1386. It strikes the hours and has no dial. Early clocks of this type were also made to stand inside the cathedral or church instead of in a bell tower. Some had models of angels or other figures to strike the hour bell, and were lighted by candles for services.

There is reliable evidence that a mechanical clock was installed in Milan in 1335. It struck the hours, and may have been the first large clock to do so. Italy probably developed striking clocks sounding the correct number of blows, soon after 1330. This improvement on the alarm, which was set to sound a bell at a certain hour and on the clock that sounded a single note at each hour, spread throughout the clockmaking centres of Europe. In 1368, three Dutch clockmakers, John and William Uneman, and John Lietuyt of Delft, were invited by King Edward III to work in England for a year and it is probable that they knew about striking clocks and made the clocks for Salisbury and for Wells Cathedrals.

There is a domestic striking clock in the museum at Nuremberg, Germany, which is said to date from 1400. If so, it is the earliest existing with hour striking as well as alarm.

Two ancient public clocks of the 14th century are still in existence in France – the Dijon clock, which is now no more than a frame, and the more complete Rouen clock, which is well authenticated. The town council of Montpelier in France had a tower with a clock keeper and 'striker of the hours by night and day', and in 1410 they became dissatisfied with their clock keeper because

he was erratic and overpaid, so they ordered one of the new clocks from Dijon which worked without a clock keeper. It had a wooden man, or 'jacquemart', that automatically struck the bell with a hammer at the hour.

England, which is richer than any other country in turret clocks of very early date, has a number of clocks with these 'jacks', i.e. mechanical figures, puppets or automata, that strike the bells or are decorative. The word 'automation' is a derivation from clock automata. Apart from the Salisbury clock, the only one without a dial, there are other very ancient clocks at Wells Cathedral, Exeter Cathedral, Ottery St. Mary Church, and Wimborne Minster. All are in the West Country, all are still working, and all have astronomical dials.

The Wells astronomical dial is one of the finest medieval dials in the world. It has a double twelve-hour ring and an early type of moon indication worked by two discs revolving at slightly different rates. At the hour, four knights on horseback have a joust and one is struck off his horse by another's lance. At the time the clock was made, knights actually fought such contests.

Outside the cathedral is another dial above which two knights in armour strike the quarters on small bells. Inside, both quarters and hours are struck by the oldest surviving jack in the world, known as 'Jack Blandifer', who kicks his heels against two bells to sound the quarters and makes determined blows with a hammer at an hour bell that hangs in front of him. The original Wells movement is in the Science Museum, London.

The oldest English clock still working in its origin[al] place is at Rye Church, in Sussex. It was made in 151[5] and was later converted to pendulum operation, but th[e] pendulum, stayed like a ship's mast, is so long that i[t] hangs down inside the church over the aisle. (There i[s] a clock in St. Chad's Church, Shrewsbury, with a pen[-] dulum over fifty-two feet long!)

During the period *c.* 1490 to 1550, English blacksmith[s] made large clocks of a different type from those of con[-] tinental design. The frame, instead of being a rectangula[r] cage, was a vertical beam with the wheels laid out in [a] line. In the West Country, the beams were of wood[,] and in the Midlands of iron. One of the best example[s] can be seen at Cothele House, Calstock, Cornwall, whic[h] belongs to the National Trust.

The escapement of all these early mechanical clock[s] is the verge (after *verga,* a wand like that carried by [a] verger in church). It is a shaft with two little 'flags' o[r] pallets attached to it. The pallets interact with the pointe[d] teeth on the edge of a special wheel, known as the 'crow[n]

LEFT: A falling ball clock of c. 1590.
It descends on the chain from which it hangs

BELOW: A 16th-century rolling or inclined plane clock that is
powered by its own weight as it slowly rolls down the slope

RIGHT: Gothic wall clock with verge and foliot control

The three clocks are in the BRITISH MUSEUM

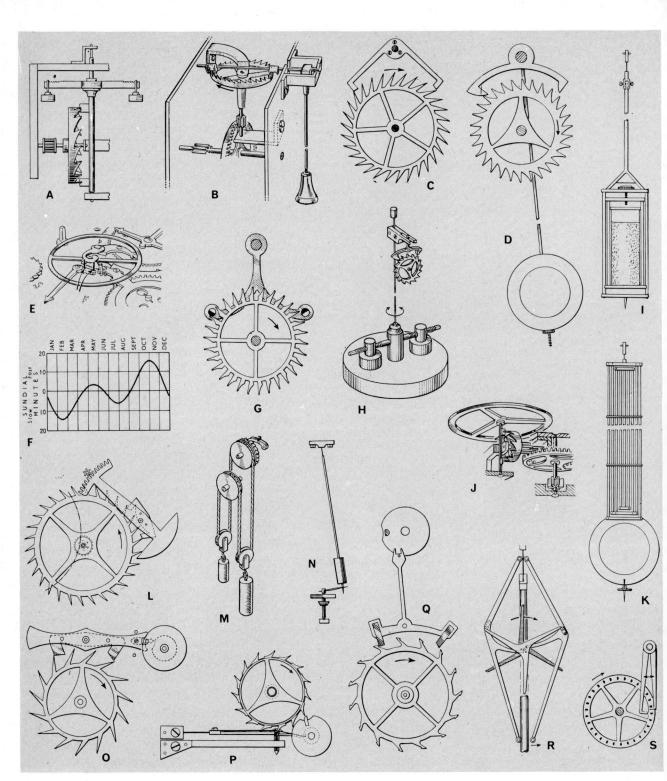

A. *The verge and foliot clock escapement, invented* c. *1300.*

B. *Verge clock escapement and bob pendulum of* c. *1700.*

C. *Graham dead beat clock escapement for accurate pendulum clocks, invented 1715.*

D. *Anchor or recoil clock escapement and pendulum invented* c. *1675.*

E. *Hogs bristle regulator for a balance wheel (shown by small arrows).*

F. *Equation of time – the difference between clock time and sundial time.*

G. *A Brocot escapement for pendulum clocks (French) of* c. *1850.*

H. *Torsion pendulum used in four-hundred-day clocks.*

I. *Graham's compensated pendulum with mercury jar,* c. *1721.*

J. *Verge watch escapement and balance wheel in use from* c. *1500*
for 300 years.

K. *Harrison's gridiron compensated pendulum* c. *1725.*

L. *Rack lever escapement for watches with balance wheels* c. *1790.*

M. *Huygens' endless rope drive of 1657, used on many later 'grandfather clocks'.*

N. *Conical pendulum and escapement in some novelty clocks.*

O. *English lever watch escapement of the 19th century.*

P. *Earnshaw's chronometer escapement,* c. *1781.*

Q. *Cole's resilient, an early lever watch escapement of* c. *1861 used* c. *1869 by Howard in America.*

R. *Grimthorpe's gravity escapement acting on Big Ben's pendulum rod.*

S. *Pin wheel escapement on French long pendulum clocks, invented 1741.*

wheel' because of its likeness to a king's crown. The driving weight of the clock turns the crown wheel as well as the dial or hand by means of gear wheels. The verge escapement restrains the crown wheel, allowing it to turn only in a series of little jumps. The little jumps cause the tick tock sounds of the clock as the verge escapement, after releasing the clock mechanism, brings it to a sudden halt by the clash of metal tooth on one or other of the pallets.

The verge escapement alone is not sufficient to make the clock run to time. It has to be combined with a time controller. The earliest was either an oscillating wheel or an oscillating bar with a weight hung at each end. This part of the mechanism is called the 'balance'. The balance in the form of a wheel, and also that called the 'foliot', which is a bar with a weight hung from each end, seem to have been invented about the same time.

The verge with foliot was used for both domestic and for large public clocks. The verge with balance wheel was for smaller clocks. A foliot or balance wheel tends to swing to and fro at a certain frequency which it tries to impose on the clock. The small weights at the ends of the foliot can be moved inwards or outwards to alter the rate. The train of gears responsible for the time-keeping was called in earlier days the 'watch train'. It has its own weight.

The 'alarm train' of a clock is separate and also has its own weight. At the time set for alarm, the alarm train is released by the watch train.

A clock which strikes has a separate 'striking train' with its own weight which is separate from other trains. It is released at each hour to strike the requisite number of blows on a bell. The number of blows is determined by a disc with slots along its edge, called a 'count wheel' or 'locking plate'. It has the same function as the part of the computer called a 'memory' or 'storage'. It remembers the sequence of blows to be struck at any hour.

As the mechanical clock was introduced into different countries from the end of the 14th century, so it changed the systems of timekeeping from the temporal hours of the sundial (with different hours for night and day, which varied throughout the year) to equal hours (which were the same day and night throughout the year).

First mechanical domestic clocks in Europe were similar to the large iron clocks, but smaller. They were from about eighteen inches to twenty-four inches high and were often hung on the wall of the central hall of the household so that the striking could be heard in other chambers. Today they are usually called 'Gothic clocks', 'chamber clocks', or 'iron clocks'.

The iron movements have four vertical corner posts, just like those of tower clocks, without protective cases. Fixed to the front, however, is usually an iron dial on which the hours and other information are painted. There are usually one or more bells on top, surmounted by a

One of the earliest musical clocks known. Made in 1598 by Nicholas Vallin, of London, a Fleming who died of the plague in 1603. It chimes on thirteen bells. The clock is in the Ilbert collection in the British Museum

spire. Time is shown by a single hour hand, or the dial turns against a stationary pointer. Gothic clocks strike the hours and sound an alarm when required. Some have dials showing the phases of the moon. The weight of the timekeeping (watch) train usually runs the clock for about six hours, so the clock has to be wound four times a day.

For about two centuries, all mechanical clocks had a weight drive like earlier water clocks. The first big impetus to the craft of clockmaking came with the invention of the coiled spring to replace the driving weight.

Invention of the spring

The clock spring revolutionised clockmaking. It was responsible for the introduction of the portable clock, and then the little clock that could be carried about on the person – that is, the watch. There is a portrait painted *c.* 1450 showing an important person of the Burgundian court who owned a spring-driven clock and was so proud of it he had it included in his picture. In 1481, King Louis XI of France paid £ 16.10s. for a clock to carry with him 'in all places where he shall go'. The first spring-driven clocks may have been Burgundian or Flemish.

In the 16th and 17th centuries, there was already a relatively large number of people in Europe who could afford to buy timekeepers, and the industry grew rapidly, particularly in Germany, where most skilled men originated because of the relatively high number of smith-gunmakers there. The first places to emerge as centres of clock and watchmaking were the towns of Augsburg and Nuremberg in South Germany.

A coiled spring replaced the weight and rope wound round a barrel which drove the clock. With one end of the length of spring attached to an arbor and coiled round it, and the other end attached to a fixed point on the movement, the spring would turn the arbor as it tried to uncoil.

Although the spring-driven clock was invented before mid-15th century, it was a long time before portable clocks came into general use. The reason was undoubtedly because of the appalling difficulty of making springs. Even two hundred years later, spring making was considered a complex task.

Because a spring will not give constant power like a weight acting under the influence of gravity, timekeeping was bad. A spring provides reducing power as it runs down and has an uneven output. Clockmakers therefore invented several devices to help. One, called 'stopwork', allows the spring to work only over a certain part of its range. The other, the 'stackfreed', is a cam which turns slowly as the mainspring runs down. A roller is pressed on the edge of the cam by a strong spring. As the mainspring runs down the friction of the stackfreed becomes less, so helping to provide even power output.

The stackfreed was a purely German device and, as the demand for Augsburg and Nuremberg clocks and watches increased, makers began using cheaper springs which had to have more compensation. So the more pronounced the snail shape of the cam, the later the timepiece.

Augsburg became particularly famous for portable clocks and its clockmakers produced an astonishing

TOP: This early clock for the bedroom opens a tinder box, fires the tinder and lights a candle which pops up

RIGHT: One of the 16th-century novelties of Augsburg, an animated negro and dog clock

The two clocks are in the BRITISH MUSEUM

variety of complicated and automata clocks during the 16th century. The earlier Augsburg clocks were drum or canister shaped with feet on the bottom and the dial on the top. Many were also made square. They are usually called 'table clocks'. A single hand shows the time of day in equal hours on a dial marked from I to XII. Under each Roman hour is another in Arabic numerals from thirteen to twenty-four. Often there is a calendar and sometimes a zodiac dial to show the ruling sign, since astrology had much influence in human affairs at that time.

A speciality of Augsburg makers was a dial held by an elephant, griffon, or other animal, with moving eyes. Another version shows a negro and his dog near a palm tree. They also made elaborate special clocks in the shape of moving ships that rolled along the table at the hour with many activities on deck, and milkmaids that milked cows, squirting real milk into a bucket.

There seemed no end to the ingenuity of the clock-makers of this town. They produced crucifix clocks in quantity, showing Christ on the Cross, a moving band at the top indicating the hour. They made monstrance clocks shaped like the ornate standing vanity mirrors of

Dial of one of the earliest known spring-driven clocks possibly made before 1500. On the outside are shown equal hours in double XII marking. Inside are shown temporal hours for different months GERMANISCHES NATIONALMUSEUM, NUREMBERG

the time, and they even invented an alarm that 'turned on the light'. At the set hour, the clock triggers a hammer carrying a flint in the same way as a flintlock musket. The sparks from the flint and the steel striking plate ignite tinder in a box that opens at the same time. The tinder lights the wick of a candle that swings upright in the box.

A typical Augsburg clock of the time is monumental in conception, having a tall ornate tower on a square base and dials on all sides. Many copies of these 'tabernacle clocks' have been made in Germany in the last century by an electro-copying technique.

Nuremberg appears to have concentrated more on watches, which are described in the next chapter.

The stackfreed was never a very practical device and while the Germans persisted with it, a much more satisfactory invention appeared in France. It was derived from an earlier invention to ease the winding of a ballister – the big catapult war machine – and is called the 'fusee', the name being derived from a word meaning 'thread'. It is a trumpet-shaped wheel with a spiral groove around it, round which is wound a length of gut (or after about 1630, in clocks, a chain). It works in this way: The free end of the gut is attached to a barrel in which a spring is wound up. As the spring barrel rotates it winds the gut around itself, pulling it off the fusee and turning the fusee. But as the gut comes off the narrow end of the fusee first, its leverage is small, when the strength of the mainspring is greatest. As the spring runs down, so the leverage of the gut on the fusee increases, to compensate.

It was such a successful device that marine chronometers and precision clocks are still being made with fusees today. There are remnants of a clock fitted with a fusee and dated 1509 in the Bavarian National Museum in Munich, but the oldest complete example is that made by Jacob the Zech, of Prague, which belongs now to the Society of Antiquaries, of London. Leonardo da Vinci made a sketch of a fusee in one of his notebooks of 1490, and there is a drawing of one for winding a ballista of 1407.

The escapement of Augsburg clocks was a verge combined with a balance wheel or bar balance, also called a 'dumb-bell balance' because it was often of that shape. The balance spring (hairspring) had not yet been invented. The clocks were regulated by two main means. The coarse adjustment was to alter the 'set-up' of the mainspring, i.e. the range over which it worked. The finer adjustment was to limit the swing of the balance. This was done by 'hog's bristle regulation'. An adjustable arm carries two short, stiff bristles against which the spoke of the balance wheel or the arms of the bar bump at the end of each swing.

The French and the Flemish made their early spring clocks of a different style and smaller size than those of the Germans. They are hexagonal, and taller than they are wide. The cases are of brass, elaborately engraved, with a domed top, underneath which is the bell, surrounded by carved frets and finials. The movements are divided into two tiers, there being three horizontal plates held together by vertical pillars.

England in the 16th century depended very largely on foreign clocks and clockmakers. Nicholas Cratzer, horologist and astronomer to King Henry VIII, was born in Bavaria in South Germany in 1487 and apparently lived in England for thirty years without learning English. Holbein, the painter, assisted him in designing clock cases. Nicolas Urseau, clockmaker and keeper to Queen Elizabeth I, was followed in that office, however, by Bartholomew Newsam, who was probably a Yorkshireman. He made spring as well as weight clocks, some of which still exist. David Ramsay, one of the most famous early makers, who became 'Clockmaker Extraordinary' to King James I, was a Scot. He was also first Master of the Worshipful Company of Clockmakers, formed under a charter obtained from King Charles I on 22nd August, 1631.

The Company was granted very extensive power to control the craft of clock and watchmaking, including

Augsburg clock with an animated griffon holding the hours dial VICTORIA & ALBERT MUSEUM, LONDON

Augsburg lion clock showing the hour at the front and quarter on the top of the case. The lion's eyes blink

the right of entry by force to premises and ships in order to destroy bad work. The object was to protect the public from persons 'making, buying, selling, transporting, and importing any bad, deceitful, or insufficient clocks, watches, larums, sun-dials, boxes, or cases for the said trade.'

The Nuremberg craft guild which was founded earlier than that in London was particularly strict and required apprentices to be trained in many skills, including working in precious metals, and being able to make astronomical dials.

The most usual domestic clock in England before 1600 was the imported iron Gothic clock, although a few immigrant clockmakers made some spring-driven table clocks of both German and French types. Some English blacksmith-clockmakers, gun founders, and lock-

LEFT: Copper gilt table clock about eighteen inches high in the form of a triumphal car which moves. It was made in Augsburg about 1600 BOWES MUSEUM, YORKSHIRE

BELOW: Early German spring-driven table clock with its original leather case. As well as showing the hours on a double XII dial it has an astrolabe with a revolving rate SOTHEBY'S, LONDON

TOP RIGHT: Top of a clock illustrating the ptolemaic system with the Earth in the centre of the universe. It also shows a calendar. The shutters below indicate times of sunrise and sunset

FAR RIGHT: Top of a clockwork model showing the Copernican system with the Earth revolving round the sun

BOTTOM RIGHT: German pistol alarm clock with a twenty-four-hour dial, c. 1600. The hammer holding the flint is released by the alarm, sparks some tow which ignites a small quantity of gunpowder to awaken the sleeper

miths copied continental iron clocks and added backs and sides of sheet iron to keep out the dust.

After about ten or so years, English makers began to use brass, or 'latten' as it was called at the time, and also reduced the size of the clock considerably. Thus the first purely English brass or latten clock appeared. Subsequently the name became changed to 'lantern clock' as the shape was something like the horn lantern of the time.

English lantern clocks are weight-driven and based on a frame made of four turned corner posts with plates at top and bottom. They stand on four feet and have four finials at the top which hold straps to take the bell on the top. The wheels and arbors of the movement are held by straps between the plates. Such a movement is said to have a 'posted frame'.

In front of the bell is a decorative brass fret showing crossed dolphins or some heraldic device. The open dial is of brass engraved with the hours in Roman figures, with engraved ornaments between them to represent half hours. The hour hand is short and stubby with a long tail so that it can be turned like a turnkey to set it to time. The tail has another purpose when the clock is fitted with an alarm. The small concentric alarm dial in the middle of the main dial can be turned so that the tail of the hour hand indicates when the alarm is to go off.

The lantern clock stood on a bracket fixed to the wall so that the driving weights could hang below it. Alternatively it was hung on the wall from a hook by means of a semi-circular stirrup on the back of the clock near the top. The bottom is kept clear of the wall by two sharp spurs on the back feet. These dig into the wall to prevent the clock from being moved sideways when it is being wound or moved by accident.

One form of lantern clock was called a 'sheepshead' because its extra large dial is supposed to have made it look like that. Another is the winged lantern clock which has glazed, fan-shaped wings on the sides. The banana-shaped pendulum hangs in the centre of the clock instead of at the back and shows first in one wing and then in the other as it swings.

All lantern clocks are weight driven and, before 1657, when the pendulum clock was invented, all of them had balance wheels, or occasionally, foliots. Few lantern clocks with their original balances still remain. Most that have survived were converted to pendulum operation at some time in their history to improve their timekeeping. Few even of these, with short pendulums,

LEFT: A late 16th-century tabernacle clock with its original leather travelling case. It is about thirteen inches tall, and has been converted to pendulum, hanging in front SOTHEBY'S, LONDON

BOTTOM LEFT: Table clocks were still made in the 18th century. This one with hour and minute hands has rack striking. It was made by Andreas Lingke of Danzig. The knob on the left is to make it repeat the hours SOTHEBY'S, LONDON

BELOW: French spring-driven table clock of the 16th century with double XII dial which also shows the phases of the moon and its age, the date and signs of the zodiac SOTHEBY'S, LONDON

RIGHT: Big automaton clock in Rosenborg Castle, Denmark. It was made in 1594 by Isaac Habrecht of Strasburg

e still to be found. Those that do remain were mostly
nverted after 1670 to, or made with, long pendulums.
 lantern clock with a metre long pendulum is an awk-
ard looking clock. It is often stood on a tapering four
ded base or trunk about four feet high to hide and
otect the pendulum. The trunk is not likely to be
iginal.

At the end of the 16th century, Augsburg and Nu-
mberg were still dominant in clock and watchmaking.
he Italian industry which had been so active in the
iddle Ages, had been largely eclipsed. From about
500 various other centres grew in strength, particu-
rly those of Blois, Paris and Lyon, in France; Geneva
 Switzerland; and London. From 1618 to 1648 the
hirty Years' War between Catholics and Protestants
srupted Germany and gradually broke up its early
ock and watchmaking industries. The forty-three master
ockmakers and the same number of journeymen in
ugsburg in 1615 had dwindled to seven in 1645. By
e 1620's, London's master clockmakers had increased
 about sixty and in the 1640's Paris had about seventy.

At this period in history, clockmaking enjoyed a very
igh standing, equivalent to electronic computer manu-
cture today. It was the first industry to apply the
eory of physics and mechanics to machines and many
ockmakers were scientists in their own right. Certainly

their intelligence was above average. They were friends
of the most advanced thinkers of the day, and their
products were not only sought after by the astronomers
and the rich and powerful, but were the basis of the
most profitable trading with the East. Sailing vessels
armed with guns gave Europe command of the seas;
clock and watches, prototypes of all precision instruments,
were the goods that opened up the Eastern markets, as
well as trade between European nations.

Because watch and clockmakers were more literate
than the rest of the population, there was probably a
higher percentage of them which followed the 16th-
century Reformation, the great religious movement led
by Luther in Germany and Zwingli in Switzerland.
Therefore the clock and watchmaking centres were most
affected by religious upheaval. The migration of a master
clockmaker at that time from one country to another
could upset the balance of industrial power in the same
way as the emigration or disaffection of an atomic scientist today.

*OP LEFT: South German rack clock of about 1600. It is driven
 its own weight, being lifted up the rack to 'wind' it*

*OP RIGHT: Dial of a German automata clock c. 1620-1630
owing the hour, date, sign of the zodiac, and phase of the moon
n the hand)* NATIONAL MUSEET, COPENHAGEN

*OTTOM LEFT: Three early small clocks. Left: a weight-driven
abernacle clock with lower dial giving information about the moon.
entre: unusual spring-driven table clock without a fusee which may
ave been made in Strasburg or Italy. Right: spring-driven table
ock, possibly Italian, with the hours marked I to XII and under
em thirteen to twenty-four. It has been converted to pendulum,
anging in front. The smallest of the three is six inches
igh* SOTHEBY'S, LONDON

*IGHT: A clock by Jeremias Metzker of Augsburg in 1564, 'missing'
or many years and recognised by Dr. F. A. B. Ward of the
cience Museum in Waddesdon Manor, Buckinghamshire in 1963.
Many electrotype copies of such clocks exist* THE NATIONAL TRUST

The story of the watch

The first watches were made in Europe – perhaps Burgundy or Flanders – not long before 1500. The iron movements were set in ball-shaped cases, like a half a dozen or so early ones that still survive, or in flat drums. At the time, so-called 'musk balls' were worn on chains or ribbons around the neck. They were decorated and perforated hollow metal spheres containing musk, used in the same way as scent is today.

A musk ball watch, sometimes wrongly called a 'Nuremberg egg' because a translator mistook *ueurlein* (little clocks) for *eierlein* (little eggs), had a small dial at the bottom similar to a pedestal foot. It was hung from the neck or kept in a purse. There was no glass and a raised rim protected the single stubby hand from damage and allowed the watch to be stood on a table on its dial when not being worn.

Nuremberg in South Germany was perhaps the earliest production centre, and Peter Henlein, a locksmith living there, is known to have been one of the first successful makers of watches, at fifteen florins each. Henlein was a quick-tempered and flamboyant character who on one occasion was responsible for the death of a man in a brawl. He had to seek refuge in the Monastery of the Barefooted Friars twenty-two times before the affair was settled with the dead man's relatives.

Blois, in France, was also known for its watches at a very early date. Julien Coudray of that town made two watches in the hilts of daggers in 1581 for the King of France.

Table clocks were reduced in size for carrying on the person. These drum or cannister-shaped watches were probably introduced about the same time as the musk ball watch. They were truly clock-watches, because they struck the hours like a clock. Because of their shape, however, they were more accurately progenitors of the pocket watch. The musk ball was a novelty.

Canister or drum watches were made in some numbers in the 16th century in Germany and had iron movements. The drive was by open mainsprings with stackfreed, verge escapement, and bar balance. The decorated case was pierced to allow the striking to be heard. It had a hinged lid which could be raised to reveal the engraved dial with its hour hand. There was no glass, but the cover was pierced so that the hours and tip of the hand could be seen without opening it. As the twenty-four-hour system of equal hours had been introduced with the clock, the dial was marked from I to XII, with

TOP: Early German clock-watch which strikes the hours. It has a stackfreed and dumb-bell balance. The top of the case is pierced to show the numerals SOTHEBY'S, LONDON

RIGHT: The earliest illustration of a watch, in an oil painting by an Italian master of c. 1560. The watch is typical mid-16th-century German. On the table is a detachable alarm mechanism for the watch, and its carrying case SCIENCE MUSEUM, LONDON

thirteen to twenty-four in Arabic numerals under each Roman one. To tell the time by touch at night a small knob was positioned at each hour.

France's centres of watchmaking extended rapidly from Blois to Paris, Lyon, Dijon, and a number of other places. They soon began to take over the lead from Germany during the Thirty Years' War. In the 16th century, France introduced the oval-shaped watch, which still had straight sides, like a tin. Towards the end of the century, both round and oval watches began to appear with rounded sides.

Geneva, in Switzerland, became a watchmaking centre some time after 1550 and London followed about 1600, both helped by Huguenots escaping religious persecution. Both centres were particularly suitable, not just because of their religious tolerance, but because they had trade fairs and export houses. Watchmakers had to depend on selling overseas to keep themselves busy. It was common for a watchmaker apprenticed in Blois, say, to go to another town often in another country, when he became a journeyman. Later, in 1685, when the Edict of Nantes protecting Protestants was revoked by King Louis XIV, hundreds of thousands of French Huguenots, including many watchmakers, fled to England and Switzerland, following those who had already established themselves abroad.

There was almost complete internationalism in the watch trade from the beginning and little resistance to new ideas or foreign craftsmen. At a later stage, when the trades became established and trade guilds were formed, foreign workmen were not so welcome and there were rebellious outbursts against the 'Straingers Artificers'.

From early days a watch was made by several crafts men. A maker would produce some parts himself, bu others, assemble the movement to his own design, hav the case made by a goldsmith, then engrave his nam and town on the watch. Parts may have been made i Blois, the watchmaker a Frenchman, and the watch mad in and labelled 'London'. Early watches with differen place names engraved on them have no national charac teristics.

More crafts were involved with watchmaking tha with clockmaking. Before 1650, the watchmaker wa supported by a jeweller, a goldsmith, an engraver, a enameller, a lapidary casemaker, and perhaps others. Th lapidary casemaker was a cutter and polisher of roc crystal. Glass over the dial had not yet been introduced so at times, part or all of the case was made of the trans parent natural quartz known as 'rock crystal'.

Enamelling was a flourishing craft in Europe lon before the watch was invented and soon became asso ciated with watch cases. Early enamelling – which is th art of melting coloured glasses on to metal – requirin special chambers in or on the surface to hold the area of different coloured glasses. These are called 'champlevé when the surface of the metal case is cut into hollows and 'cloisonné' when little strips of metal form the com partments for the enamel. Both were used on earl watches. A method of painting pictures on a whit ground in enamels without the cells, discovered by French goldsmith, Jean Toutin, working in Blois abou 1630, made enamelling particularly suitable for watch cases, and gave a big impetus to Blois, which was alread specialising in cases. Blois enamels on watch case frequently picture flowers, and less often scenes an

*An 'uhrlein'
(small clock or watch) in
a canister case, made by Caspar
Werner in 1548. Note the
stackfreed and the dumb-bell balance*
WUPPERTALER UHRENMUSEUM,
W. GERMANY

portraits. Some of the finest Blois work was done in the fifteen or so years before 1650.

Enamelling was also practiced in London, Paris, and Geneva. Geneva became a main centre in the 17th century. The most famous enamellers working there was the family of Huaud, whose work often depicted buxom and women with old men staring through prison bars. Geneva still has its enamellers today, but on a small scale compared with the past, particularly in the 19th century, when the craft was at its height there.

Most early watches were highly regarded as jewels, probably before their timekeeping qualities. Their time-keeping was not good; it could easily be half an hour or more out. Nevertheless, there was a reaction against decoration in England in Puritan times, and a particularly small watch in the shape of a flattened egg was introduced some time before 1650. It has been labelled the 'Puritan watch'.

Being Calvinistic, Geneva ignored sumptuary laws and made rock crystal and metal cases in all shapes and forms imitating birds, flowers, animals, books, skulls, and other objects, known as 'form watches'. Many were fine, but some crudely made. Cutting rock crystal was a speciality of the town as early as mid-16th century. In the 17th century, Geneva became well known for its 'Abbess watches' made in the form of crosses in rock crystal.

The biggest technical change in watches occurred soon after 1675 when the balance spring, or hairspring, was introduced. This did much the same for the watch as the pendulum did for the clock, increasing its accuracy to an exceptional degree in a single jump. The pendulum has the force of gravity acting as a spring continuously pulling it into the zero position. The hairspring does the

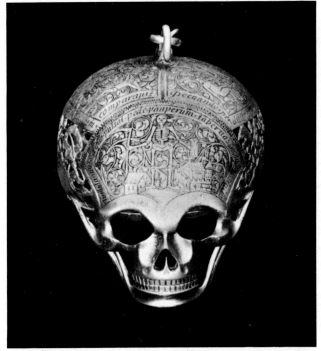

LEFT: *Small but complicated English watch of c. 1600 by J. Burgis. Hours at the bottom. The top dial shows date, month and sign of the zodiac. On the right is moon dial*

TOP RIGHT: *Star-shaped form watch by David Ramsay, c. 1600. Ramsay was first Master of the Worshipful Company of Clockmakers in 1632. The watch is worn round the neck by Masters today*
WORSHIPFUL COMPANY OF CLOCKMAKERS, LONDON

RIGHT: *French-made silver skull watch as big as a boy's fist. To see the time it is held upside down and the jaw hinged open. It is reported to have been given to Mary Seton by Mary Queen of Scots before her execution in 1585*
WORSHIPFUL COMPANY OF CLOCKMAKERS, LONDON

same for a watch, pulling the hairspring into the central position. Both Robert Hooke in England and Christiaan Huygens in Holland, who is now given the credit, claimed the invention.

New watches were made with hairsprings and old ones were converted in thousands. The improved time-keeping with the balance and hairspring also meant the rapid introduction of another hand, the minute hand.

By chance, the long waiscoat came into fashion in England about the same time as the hairspring and the pendant watch disappeared into the waistcoat pocket. (We still call the loop on a pocket watch 'the pendant'). As the watch was now more often hidden it became less decorative and more practical during the last quarter of the 17th century.

Reading the hours and minutes indicated by two moving hands on a fixed circular dial was still novel to most people in the 17th century. It was not taught to children as a normal part of their upbringing, nor was it universal in all countries, as it is today. It was thought therefore by some watchmakers that there might be a more practical way of indicating time and, around 1700, there were many experiments to this end, before the watch settled down to two or three hands and a cir-cular dial.

It is safe to say that every novelty watch dial that appears today has an ancestor in some clock or watch of the past. One of the experiments in about 1700, re-peated at frequent intervals subsequently, was what is now called 'digital indication', as it showed the hour and minutes as numbers in apertures, thus: 11.52.

The wandering hour watch, another experiment, was inspired by the night clocks of the time. An hour nu-meral moved around a semi-circular opening during th course of an hour and its position in the semi-circle in dicated the minutes. As one hour disappeared on th right another appeared on the left. The dial was onl half as accurate as a normal one.

A variation was the 'Sun and Moon watch.' In thi the semi-circular opening in the dial was marked roun the edge with twelve hours, starting at VI through t XII and on again to VI. At six in the morning, a smal image of the sun appeared and moved round the hour during the day, disappearing at VI on the right of th dial, when a moon appeared on the left to mark the nigh hours. It could not be read very accurately because c the small spaces between the hour marks, so on som a minute hand was also provided.

There were watches with twenty-four-hour dials, an others with dials laid out in the same way as regulato clocks, the hour, minute and second hands havin separate rings of numbers. Some watches had six-hou dials. The idea was that as the minute hand moved twic as fast as a normal one, it could be read twice as accu rately. Later watches appeared with hands that move through a semi-circle to mark the hours, then jumpe back to zero when they reached the end of the scale which represented twelve o'clock. After the French Rev olution, there was an attempt to introduce a differen time system based on two periods of ten hours instea of two periods of twelve during a day, and ten instea of twelve months in the year. Some decimal watches wer

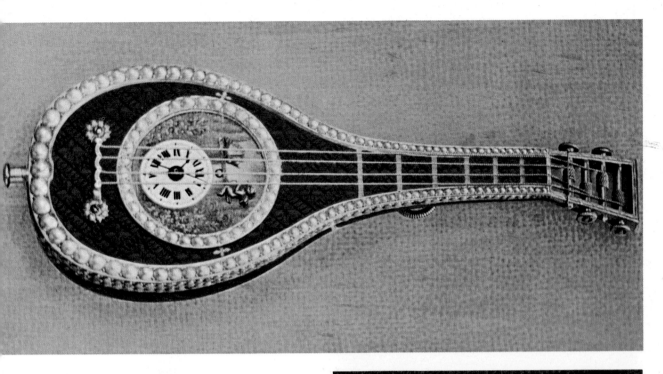

Before the hairspring provided good timekeeping, novelty came first. This crazy dial watch was made c. 1670 *by Robertus Wood of London. The outer case is of tortoiseshell*

'Sun and Moon' dial by Trubshaw. The time shown by the sun and minute hand is two minutes after four o'clock in the afternoon. A moon indicates night hours SOTHEBY'S, LONDON

Wandering hour watch by Vaucher Frères showing thirty-eight minutes past ten. The key, which will only wind one way, is called a 'tipsy key'

made, with ten-hour dials, usually accompanied by normal markings.

A number of the earliest watches of the 16th century had additional complications to indicate the phase of the moon, the day of the month, even the day of the week, the sign of the zodiac, and other information considered useful at the time.

Because the pendulum was so successful as a regulator for the clock, a few watchmakers, not understanding the principles involved, made watches with pendulums, which were hopeless timekeepers. At the same time, they caught the imagination of buyers of watches. More commercially minded watchmakers in England and Holland (where the pendulum was invented), made 'pendulum watches' that had a little disc attached to the balance wheel. In the English ones, the balance wheel was positioned under the dial instead of on the back of the movement and the disc could be seen swinging to and fro, like a mock pendulum, through an aperture in the dial.

Some magnificent engraved cases in gold were produced during the 18th century and also cases set with ornamental stones and gems. Because enamelled cases in particular, were works of art and could be damaged and also because they were made by a separate craftsman, the watch was not fitted directly into the enamelled case. Instead it was in a plain case of gold which fitted into the enamelled one. A third protective case enclosed the enamelled one.

In the 18th century, the English became the most dominant watchmaking nation, leading the French and the Swiss. The English trade was centred on London, many watchmakers working in the Fleet Street district. Most made clocks as well as watches. One reason why the English gained the ascendancy was the introduction of more efficient working methods. Thomas Tompion (1639-1713) most famous of all clock and watchmakers, produced about six thousand watches at the rate of three or four a week, and about five hundred and fifty clocks. It has been estimated that ninety per cent of the time spent in his workshops was on watches. He organised the workshop in a new way, which anticipated the methods of the Industrial Revolution by two centuries. His methods were described by Sir William Pettey, greatest political economist of the 17th century, in these words: 'In the making of a Watch, if one Man shall make the *Wheels*, another the *Spring*, another shall Engrave the *Dial-plate*, and another shall make the *Cases*, then the *Watch* will be better and cheaper, than if the whole Work be put upon any one Man.' Tompion introduced 'engines' for cutting wheel teeth to replace hand-cutting.

The English also led in technical innovation. George Graham, who worked with Tompion, became his son-in-law and his successor, developed the horizontal, or cylinder escapement, an improvement on the verge. He sent one to Julien Le Roy in France who was so impressed with it that it became much more used by the French and the Swiss than the English.

In 1770, Thomas Mudge, from Exeter, a magnificent craftsman who always refused to charge high prices, made a watch for Queen Charlotte. This contained a lever escapement, which he invented for clocks in 1754. A year after he finished the Queen Charlotte watch, Mudge left his business and went to live in Plymouth to devote his life to marine timekeepers. A few years later he wrote in a letter about the lever escapement: 'whoever would rob me of it does me an honour.' Yet this escapement was more successful than any other and is still by far the most important today, having been used in countless millions of timekeepers.

Mudge in fact developed an earlier escapement called the rack lever, invented by the Abbé d'Hautefeuille in 1722 and based on a clock escapement by George Graham. He turned it into a detached lever. From 1782, Josiah Emery, Grant, Pendleton, Perigal, Dutton, and John Leroux made lever watches, but they were not good enough to compete with the English pocket chronometers of the last quarter of the 18th century. These employed the detent escapement developed by John Arnold and Thomas Earnshaw for the marine chronometer. Also, in 1782, the duplex escapement was patented in England. It had been invented by Pierre Le Roy in France and was taken up enthusiastically by English makers as a cheaper and more robust alternative to the detent escapement, which it resembled.

Commercial development of the lever watch occurred in a remarkable way. Peter Litherland, a maker in Liverpool in the north west of England, set up a factory for making watches by semi-mass production methods. His watches incorporated the original rack lever escapement of the Abbé d'Hautefeuille. They were better than the cheap verge escapement watches of the time, made in London and the continent. His designs and methods were adopted by other Liverpool makers, who built up an export trade to America from the last years of the 18th century.

Then in 1815, year of Napoleon's defeat at Waterloo, Edward Massey of Liverpool independently repeated what Mudge had done and invented the detached lever escapement. It was, however, a much better version than Mudge's. Five years later the London makers had to take notice of the lever because it was beginning to rival the chronometer escapement and was less liable to disturbance. After mid-19th century, the English lever became the chief escapement for high quality as well as cheaper watches. There was another escapement

Watch by Thomas Tompion of Water Lane, Fleet Street, in a silver pair case. Tompion was probably the first to make watches by a form of batch production, in the 18th century
MR. T. P. CAMERER CUSS, LONDON

The first lever watch, made by Thomas Mudge for Queen Charlotte in 1770. It has a centre seconds hand

ABOVE: Farmer's watch, a cheap product of the 19th century

RIGHT: English watch of 1805-1806 with English enamelled case in Joshua Reynolds style
WILSDORF COLLECTION AT ROLEX WATCHES, GENEVA

OPPOSITE: Bilston boxes. These fine painted and fired enamel boxes were made from 1760 to 1830 in the small town of Bilston in south Staffordshire, England, following the style of the earlier Battersea enamels. Some were real watch cases, but many were sham watches of varying degrees of realism as shown above. 1 and 7, real watches in Bilston enamel cases, marked 'fres Esquivillon & Dechoudens' and 'Thos. Thomas, London' respectively. 4 and 10, Bilston sham watches with false winding mechanism and movable hands. They open just like real verge watches, but there is nothing inside except a polished steel mirror behind which is the winding mechanism. 2,8 and 9, Bilston sham watches with movable hands – hinged boxes with glasses. 11, Bilston sham watch made from a hinged box with painted hands and a glass. 5, Bilston sham watch from a hinged box with painted hands and no glass. 3, 12, and 13 Bilston toy watches – painted closed boxes. 6, Bilston watch key made from a closed box COLLECTION: CHARLES TERWILLIGER, BRONXVILLE, NEW YORK, USA

commonly used for cheaper watches in the Lancashire town of Ormskirk. It is called the 'Ormskirk escapement' or the 'chaff-cutter', because the double escape wheel looked like a chaff-cutter, and was based on a French invention.

Another reason for the dominance of the English watch was its jewelled bearings that reduced friction and wear. They were introduced by a Swiss protégé of Sir Isaac Newton. He was Nicolas Facio, who with two watchmakers, Peter and Jacob Debaufre, from France, applied for a patent for piercing jewels. (Facio also had a scheme for the raising of the dead!) Later the patent was rejected by Parliament after a petition was presented by English watchmakers. The Worshipful Company of Clockmakers offered as evidence 'an old watch' by Ignatius Huggeford with a working jewel made before the patent. In more recent times it was discovered that the jewel in this watch is false, probably put there for decoration or as false evidence. No one will ever know. The watch can be seen in the Clockmakers Company Museum in the Guildhall, London. At any rate, London watchmakers kept the secret of drilling precious stones for watch bearings for many years.

KEY		
1	2	3
4	5	6
7	8	9
10	11	12	13

The outer case of this watch by Robert Seignor is piqué – that is, of leather decorated by gold pins MR. T. P. CAMERER CUSS, LONDON

LEFT: *Automata watch of about 1770 which, when a button is pressed, shows a man plucking a fiddle and a woman playing a harp while a dancer emerges* WUPPERTALER UHRENMUSEUM, W. GERMANY

BOTTOM LEFT: *Watch of* c. *1790 for astronomers by George Margetts, of London showing hours, minutes and seconds of mean time and, by the inner rotating dials, of sidereal or star time*

BELOW: *Japanese striking watch of* c. *1790 in an 'inro' case, a small wooden box normally used for carrying medicines. It is fastened to the kimono girdle by the cords and netsuke (button)*

OPPOSITE: *A-L. Breguet, a Swiss who worked in France, and became probably the most famous watchmaker of all time*

Watches generally were wound by using a separate key until after mid-19th century. Some ingenious keyless winding systems were invented, but that eventually adopted was by using a winding button. One early idea was 'pump winding' by a plunger which also carried the watch bow.

Over the last quarter of the 18th century and until 1823, French watchmakers enjoyed the enormous prestige of a Swiss-born watchmaker working in Paris, who is often called today the finest watchmaker of all time. His name was Abraham-Louis Breguet and the firm he founded still exists. He changed the appearance of the watch from the fat, rather clumsy, pocket watch to a slim, gold, quite plain watch that still looks modern. Before Breguet's time, French watches were thicker than English ones. Earlier, until about 1720, they were so fat, they were generally known as 'oignons' (onions).

Breguet watches today fetch very much higher prices than in his lifetime. One was sold at Sotheby's auction rooms in London in 1965 for £ 27,500. It had been made by Breguet for Junot, one of Napoleon's generals.

He started the fashion of engine-turned decoration – fine geometrical incised patterns – for gold cases, and dials, and his inventions included a shock-absorbing device to protect the balance, now used in almost every watch. He developed the self-winding pocket watch that had been invented in Switzerland by Perrelet and patented in London by Recordon. He adopted the lever escapement and improved it, but failed to take the development to the limit. He also invented an ingenious revolving escapement called a 'tourbillon' that eliminated positional errors in a pocket watch. (All watches will run at different rates in different positions).

As so many of his watches were faked, he used to place a tiny secret signature on some of them. This can just be seen by the twelve on enamel dials and either side of the twelve on metal ones. Breguet made a series called 'souscription watches', which were simple and large watches with enamel dials and single hands. They were subscribed to in advance, the object being to provide watches of the highest possible quality but at a low price.

At this time the French generally led in fashionable watches, but the English precision watches were best. The Swiss followed the French lead and gradually overhauled them in the 19th century. Geneva became the leading centre of enamelling. Large numbers of novelty watches were made by the Swiss. They included musical watches that played a tune at will, and automaton watches that showed animated scenes, such as a revolving water mill or windmill, two cherubs on a swing, a woman at a spinning wheel, men sawing, or a waterfall flowing. Some had pornographic scenes, revealed by pressing a secret button.

The Swiss also returned to the form watches that

they had made so successfully in an earlier century, imitating musical instruments – harps and mandolins were favourites – animals, vases, etc., but now they were usually colourfully enamelled over an engine-turned or engraved surface.

They were also busy technically and in 1776 invented the dead-beat seconds hand, that jumped every second and could be stopped without stopping the watch. It was the forerunner of the stop watch and the chronograph.

About 1850, both English and Swiss watches trades flourished in the export markets, with the English ahead. The English basic watch had a fusee and lever escapement. The Swiss one was cheaper, employing a cylinder escapement and a going barrel, which also helped to make it thinner. Both industries depended on hand finishing methods. But new ideas, fresh advances on Liverpool's lead, were being tried out by Frederic Japy in Switzerland, and by a number of pioneers in North America. Biggest production advances were made by the North Americans as described in Chapter 7.

The Swiss adopted and adapted the American methods. The English refused to. There were about eighty thousand watchmakers in the industry in the 19th century

in England and when a factory was set up in Soh Birmingham, to make watches by machine, it wa smashed by handworkers who thought their jobs threa ened. In the 1850's, the trade flourished in Clerkenwe (London), Prescot (Lancashire), and Coventry (whe watchmakers were superior craftsmen and wore whit aprons and top hats). In less than fifty years nothing wa left of the whole industry but one watch factory, Rothe hams of Coventry (now finished) and one chronomet factory, Thomas Mercer of St. Albans (now the world biggest). After the Second World War, the industry wa restarted with government aid by Smiths, Ingerso the armament people, Vickers (who soon withdrew and Newmark (who changed to electronics at a late stage). Two American firms were also established i Scotland.

The English remained inventive, despite the earli commercial disaster. In 1894, B. Bonniksen produced

. J. Cole, one of the finest later English
atchmakers, was called 'The English Breguet'
cause his style was similar, as in
is watch of c. 1820

Complicated watch
made by Girard Perrégaux of
Switzerland for Spain in 1880. It gives
time of day, date, and phase of the moon

Movement of one of the first self-winding
'pedometer watches', by Recorden, Spencer
and Perkins of London, c. 1780.
The fish-shaped weight bounces and winds
the spring as the wearer walks

implified version of the tourbillon he called the 'karru-
el'. John Harwood, an Englishman from Lancashire, pat-
nted the first self-winding wrist watch in 1924, and
et up factories for making it in Switzerland and America.
ut he was ahead of his time. The slump of 1931 killed
he enterprise and the self-winding watch did not become
opular until his patents had run out.

The wrist watch itself was very late on the scene for
eneral use, although Queen Elizabeth I had one, and
everal examples of the 17th century are known. Wrist
atches were considered not too practical for women
nd too effeminate for men. During the First World War,
owever, officers of opposing armies discovered that a
rist watch was much more serviceable than a pocket
atch that had to be extracted from under a Sam Brown
r webbing. The wrist watch strap with a leather cup
o hold a small pocket watch was introduced about the
urn of the century, but in 1906, a London saddler,

Alfred E. Pearson, had the idea of soldering wire loops
to watch cases to which straps could be attached.

The English lever escapement was adopted by the
Swiss but with a modification devised by Breguet to the
teeth of the escape wheel. This semed to be the ultimate
development of the watch until suddenly in the 1950's
it became known that several firms were secretly developing an electric watch, particularly the French concern,
Lip. But it was the Hamilton Watch Co. of America
that was first, in 1957. In the Hamilton electric watch,
the mainspring is eliminated and replaced by a tiny
battery that lasts about eighteen months. The balance
wheel is also a motor that drives the hands and the
timekeeping is very good, although the principle of
keeping the balance free from interference was challenged.

In 1960, an even more dramatic development
occurred. The balance wheel as well as the mainspring
was eliminated in the Accutron watch invented by a

Montre à tact' – a watch for telling the time
the dark or for blind people. The outer
and is turned until it stops and indicates
gainst small knobs on the edge of the case
OTHEBY'S, LONDON

Because keys were lost, experiments were made
with keyless winding. One system was pump
winding, by pressing the knob on top as in
this gold watch of 1816 by Massey of London
MR. T. P. CAMERER CUSS, LONDON

Souscription watch by Breguet
et Fils, Paris. It was an attempt
to provide highest quality at
reasonable prices
SOTHEBY'S, LONDON

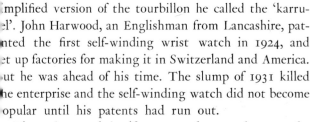

Swiss, Max Hetzel, and developed by the Bulova Watch Co., in the USA. A tuning fork about an inch long replaces the balance wheel and drives the hands by a remarkable miniature pawl and ratchet wheel turning thirty-eight million times a year. The watch hums quietly (on note E) instead of ticking. The tuning fork is kept in vibration by a battery operating a miniature oscillating circuit. Timekeeping is exceptionally good and remains so through the life of the watch. These movements are used for time switches in artificial satellites. Incidentally, Breguet's firm in Paris made tuning fork clocks in 1867.

Inventors in Britain, France, and elsewhere, are working on a radio watch that is kept to time by a continuous radio time signal, but the problem not yet overcome is preventing the watch from losing when cut off from the signals, such as when the wearer is in a steel lift or elevator. Most concentrated research is being carried out by the Swiss on miniaturised electronic circuits for watches which depend on a quartz crystal for their timekeeping element, and eventually, it is hoped, will have no moving parts. Clocks of this type have already been developed by the Germans. A quartz-crystal electronic watch with moving hands appeared in a top position in the Neuchâtel Observatory tests in 1967.

In recent years, the Japanese and the Russian watch industries have been challenging the Swiss in mechanical watch production. Both have developed very large scale production by limiting the number of models and by introducing new production methods. America also remains a big producer of lower priced watches, but the Swiss are still unassailable for special and higher quality watches.

Clocks grow up

It was in the 17th-century climate of expanding trade and high standing of clockmaking that a huge stride was made in clock accuracy.

It had long been known that a pendulum would keep better time than a foliot or balance wheel, but no one had managed to harness one to a clock movement. In 1581, a young man of seventeen years called Galileo watched a large lamp swinging in the Cathedral at Pisa, in Italy. He timed it against his pulse and recorded that it kept the same time whether swinging in a small or a large arc. He found that the time of swing depended only on the length of a pendulum.

This discovery persuaded astronomers to time astronomical phenomena by counting the swings of a weight suspended from a cord. Hevelius, of Danzig, one of the greatest 17th-century astronomers, used his pulse for timing, and also had water clocks that showed minutes, but he records: 'I was never able to find any clock, even one with a double balance, which completely avoided all irregularities.'

The clock with the double balance, now known as the 'cross-beat' was invented by a Swiss clockmaker and mathematician named Jobst Burgi, who worked for the famous astronomer Tycho Brahe and his equally famous assistant Johannes Kepler. It had two arms which swung in opposite directions across each other.

After reading of Galileo's discovery, Hevelius frequently employed cord pendulums and counted the swings to time observations. He also employed clockmakers to work on his ideas of making an automatic counting device — in other words, a pendulum clock — and eventually succeeded in making two, one of which was given to Casimir, King of Poland. He was, however, too late with his invention.

Galileo, too, in his old age pondered on the problem and actually solved it when he was seventy-seven years old and totally blind. He told his son, Vincenzio, the solution, stressing the need for secrecy. Vincenzio started to make a pendulum clock himself, then his father died and he forgot the task until seven years later, when he engaged a locksmith to carry out some work while he himself made the secret escapement by which the pendulum could be applied to the mechanism.

Only the hands and the gearing to operate them – the 'motion work' – remained to be applied when Vincenzio was attacked by a fever from which he died, but not before, in his delirium he had smashed all his clocks but this one. He also left a drawing of the pendulum and escapement invented by his father.

The existence of the drawing was unknown until about eighty years later when an Italian professor noticed that his meat was wrapped in some pages of an old manuscript. He identified them as writing in Latin by Galileo and at once hurried to the butcher to recover as many as were left of the rest of the documents. The butcher had bought them by weight as wrapping paper from the nephew of a man named Viviani, who had been a friend of Galileo. On Galileo's death, Viviani had been given the documents, but had hidden them in the bottom on a bin of grain at his home in Florence because he feared they might incriminate him in some way owing to Galileo's unpopularity with the church.

A pendulum clock was invented by accident when two brothers living in Rome, Giuseppe and Matteo Campani, who were telescope makers, were asked to make a silent clock for use at night. Giuseppe, who dabbled in clocks, experimented with one that had a vertical foliot. He increased the length of the foliot arm and stuck lumps of lead on the ends with sealing wax. He wrote, about this: 'While I was watching the action, the upper weight fell off, leaving only the lower weight, and to my astonishment, the clock continued to work, with the balance out of equilibrium, and I found the going extremely regular.'

Giuseppe Campani fitted a similar pendulum to a watch and found it went well if hung up. (Obviously he did not appreciate that the portability of the watch was destroyed by using a pendulum in it). He showed it to the Grand Duke Ferdinand II who produced a print showing the pendulum invention of the Dutchman, Christiaan Huygens.

Kochanski, mathematician to the King of Poland, also discovered the same thing by accident. He wrote: 'I had obtained a watch in which half the balance, consisting of two spoon-like arms, was broken away. I noticed that the remaining half oscillated rapidly, but nevertheless uniformly. I then remembered Galileo's pendulum which he had used for measuring time.' After this discovery, Kochanski attached a piece of natural magnet (lodestone) to the balance and claimed invention of the magnetic watch in 1659.

Preceding these claims by a very substantial period are drawings made in sketchbooks of 1452 to 1519 by Leonardo da Vinci showing pendulums with crown and verge escapements, but these were for pump mechanisms.

In the meantime the problem had been satisfactorily

Longcase clock with black lacquer case nine feet high, made about 1730 by William Hawkins of Bury St. Edmunds

*Thomas Tompion, the most famous
of all English clock and watch makers*

olved by the great Dutch scientist and astronomer, Chrisiaan Huygens, a bachelor who was also a fine painter, engraver, *littérateur*, and musician. He arrived at the solution by a mathematical analysis and some brilliant mechanics. Galileo's statement that a pendulum swung from side to side in the same time, regardless of the angle of its swing, was, Huygens said, only absolutely correct if the pendulum swung through a steeper path than an arc, called a 'cycloidal curve'.

He worked out a way of applying the verge escapement to the pendulum, a method of supending the pendulum so that it would swing in a cycloidal curve, a method of linking it to the verge, and a way of driving by weights so that the timekeeping would not be affected while the clock was being wound. On earlier weight driven (and spring-driven) clocks, the power was removed by the action of winding, which stopped the clock or made it lose time.

Huygens' winding system was subsequently used in nearly all longcase clocks that had to be wound daily. It is employed today for automatic electric winding for both modern and ancient turret clocks.

The first pendulum clock was made to Huygens' design by a clockmaker called Salomon Coster, of The Hague, in 1657. In 1658 Huygens' book describing it, *Horologium*, was published. It was the drawing in this book that the Grand Duke Ferdinand showed to Giuseppe Campani.

Hevelius also saw the book and congratulated Huygens on beating him to the invention of the pendulum clock. The reaction to the book in Italy was somewhat different. According to the 1662 minutes of the Accademia del Cimento, certain scientists claimed the invention as Galileo's. In a later edition is an engraving purporting to be Galileo's invention. It shows a clock looking rather like a garden sundial with a pendulum hanging below it. Galileo's papers were not then known to exist, having been hidden by Viviani, but when the true drawing of the escapement came to light, it showed the Academy of Sciences drawing to be an obvious fake.

At this point an incredible rapid transfer of information occurred that was responsible for making England the dominant clock and watch producing nation for almost all the next two centuries. In the same year as Huygens published his book *Horologium*, a clockmaker of Dutch extraction in London, Ahasuerus Fromanteel, published an advertisement in the *Mercurius Politicus* of

TOP RIGHT. Clock reputed to have been given by King Henry VIII to Anne Boleyn at their marriage in 1532. Queen Victoria bought it from Horace Walpole's effects in 1842, and it is now in the library at Windsor Castle

RIGHT: Winged lantern clock. The end of the banana-shaped pendulum bob can be seen on the left MR. ERNEST L. EDWARDES, SALE

27th October, 1658 and in the *Commonwealth Mercur[y]* of 25th November, 1658, which announced:

'There is lately a way found out for making clock[s] that to exact and keep equaller time than any now mad[e] without this Regulator (examined and proved before h[is] Highness the Lord Protector by such Doctors whos[e] knowledge and learning is without exception)...'

The Lord Protector was Oliver Cromwell and th[e] Regulator was the pendulum. How did Ahasuerus Fro[-]manteel begin making pendulum clocks within month[s] of Huygens' invention at a time when it took *years* fo[r] simple ideas to spread only fifty or a hundred miles fro[m] London, and quarter of a century or more for most idea[s] to cross the English Channel?

Huygens assigned the right of making his pendulum clocks to Salomon Coster for twenty-one years. One o[f] the Fromanteel family, John, was serving his apprentice[-]ship in London and was sent to The Hague to work fo[r] Coster only eleven days after the patent was granted[.] Ahasuerus, being of Dutch extraction, must have ha[d] some excellent lines of communication.

Huygens' design had much more far reaching in[-]fluence than just the pendulum because it, in effec[t] turned the table clock on its side so that the two plates[,] joined by pillars, were front and back instead of being top and bottom. However, his proposal to use 'cycloida[l] cheeks' to make the pendulum swing in a cycloidal curv[e] instead of the arc of a circle, was considered to be un[-]necessary.

Most clockmakers omitted the cheeks and attache[d] the ten-inch pendulum rod directly to the horizonta[l] verge arbor, as in Leonardo da Vinci's sketches of 1452[-]1519! The verge arbor was pivotted in a hole at the fron[t] and had 'knife edge suspension', a v-shaped piece of stee[l] rocking on a plate like a weighing machine, at the back of the clock where the pendulum hung. The pendulum bob was a pear-shaped brass nut that screwed on the bottom of the pendulum rod. Screwing it down a bi[t] slows the clock and screwing it up makes the clock g[o] faster. Since it was difficult at the time to cut an inside thread in the bob, a hole was drilled through it and a plug of pearwood pressed in and also drilled. The thread on the rod, when screwed in, cut a thread in the pearwood[.]

Fromanteel and almost all the London clockmakers rapidly adopted the clock with the short pendulum[.] There were two main versions, one weight-driven and

TOP LEFT: English dial clock with an eight-day movement by James Wilson, of Broad Court. The dial is about one foot four inches in diameter BIGGS OF MAIDENHEAD

LEFT: Bracket clock by Thomas Hill of Fleet Street on its original wall bracket, which is unusual as it slides on to a frame fixed to the wall GARRARD & CO., CROWN JEWELLERS, LONDON

he other spring-driven. The first weight clocks were
hung on the wall like the lantern clock, from which they
were a derivation, but they had plate instead of pillar
movements and wooden instead of brass cases. Weights
hung below them. They are called 'hooded wall clocks'.

Spring-driven pendulum clocks were similar in construction with wooden cases and stood on a wall bracket
or on the table. The style was classical, that is architectural in the Greek style, like the Parthenon, with a triangular
shaped top and a pillar at each side and the case of ebony
veneer.

The case became separate from the clock movement
– in the lantern clock it was a part of the clock – and
cabinet makers joined the horological industry. The
pendulum increased the accuracy of clocks from a quarter
of an hour to minutes and was responsible for the universal
introduction of minute hands.

About 1660 another form of wooden clock appeared
that was to transform the English trade. Someone, perhaps Fromanteel or Edward East, placed the wooden
cased weight-driven wall clock on a long trunk standing
on the floor to enclose the weights, and the English longcase clock was born. This was not the first clock ever
to have a long case. Isolated earlier examples exist by
continental makers, but without pendulums, of course.

The name 'grandfather clock' did not appear until
the song, *'My grandfather's clock was too tall for the shelf...'*
written by Henry Clay Work in 1876. He was an American
and was said to have been inspired by a longcase clock
in the George Hotel, Piercebridge, North Yorkshire, that
stopped on the death of its owner. Shelf clocks were
popular in America at the time he wrote. The longcase
clock has also been called the 'tall clock' and the 'coffin
clock'.

The first longcase clocks had architectural tops and
narrow trunks and were only about six feet six inches
high, which is short by later standards. The pendulum
could not be seen in the trunk with the weights as it
was short, like those on spring-driven bracket clocks.

About 1670 came an invention that released the full
potential of the pendulum, a new escapement to replace
the verge and crown wheel that had ruled for five centuries and was to continue for another century in watches.
It was called the 'anchor' because an anchor-shaped
device replaced the flag-like pallets of the verge arbor.

The anchor escapement worked in conjunction with a

*TOP RIGHT: Regency carriage clock in the French style, made
between 1815 and 1824 by N. Hart and Sons of Cornhill,
London* BIGGS OF MAIDENHEAD

*RIGHT: A coaching clock of the later 17th century by Daniel Quare.
It is four and a half inches in diameter. There is a swivel below
the pendant for it to be hung on a hook in a coach or chaise*
JAMES ROBINSON INC., NEW YORK

ABOVE: Louis XVI ormulu mantel clock of about 1760
BIGGS OF MAIDENHEAD

LEFT: French style of cartel clock, but made by Stennett of Bath, England, about 1775. The case is of gilded wood
BIGGS OF MAIDENHEAD

RIGHT: Elaborate French longcase clock with a long pendulum which can be seen through the glass in the case BIGGS OF MAIDENHEAD

FAR RIGHT: Extraordinary French astronomical clock by Passemant and Danthiou, which chimes, repeats the hour, and gives mean and solar time, information about the sun and moon, and orbital motions of five planets. It was finished in 1749 after twenty years of planning

toothed wheel which had its thirty teeth around the edge like any other toothed wheel instead of on the side of the band like the crown wheel. It was the verge and crown wheel 'straightened out' so that the wheel and its teeth and the pallets were all in the same plane.

Robert Hooke, the brilliant and irascible first experimenter of the Royal Society, may have suggested the idea. The earliest existing clock with an anchor and pendulum escapement is in the Science Museum, London and was made by William Clement for King's College, Cambridge, in 1671.

It was found that a pendulum about thirty-nine inches long swung from one side to the other in one second. The pendulum was suspended from a short length of spring instead of a thread. It was employed with a thirty tooth escape wheel because the wheel would jump forwards half a tooth every second and make one full rotation in one minute. A hand on the end of the arbor carrying this wheel therefore became a seconds hand. Almost all longcase clocks with long pendulums have seconds hand in the upper half of the dial.

The longcase clock became a valuable article of furniture during the period from 1670 to the beginning of the 19th century, when large numbers were made. To have a clock with a long pendulum was at first something of social distinction and the middle of the door of the case often had a circular or oval glass set in it so that the pendulum could be seen.

After about 1700, the longcase clock movement became more or less standardised. London makers concentrated on them in preference to spring-driven clocks until nearly 1750, when the output of provincial makers all over Great Britain and Ireland, particularly in Lancashire and Yorkshire, swamped that of London. Makers in London applied themselves more to the bracket clock after about 1750

Cases of longcase clocks went through a sequence of fashions associated with furniture. They also grew bigger and more important looking. Little is known of the case cabinet makers, and the clockmaker whose name appeared on the dial was often more of a workmaster because in London, particularly, the clockmaking industry was turning over to production in batches instead of making individual clocks.

Earliest cases had carcases of oak covered with ebony veneer, or were of pearwood stained black. Olivewood and walnut veneers followed. Veneers were also laid in geometrical patterns called 'parquetry', and elaborate floral, bird, or seaweed patterns, called 'marquetry'. In the same period, near the start of the 18th century, there was also a fashion for lacquered or japanned cases. Lacquering was an eastern art imitated in Europe. The ground colour was usually blue, green, or red, on which were painted eastern designs in blues, reds, greens and gold. Burr walnut veneers continued in favour, but after imports of mahogany were permitted from the 1740's, most better cases were made of this.

Cheaper clocks and those for more businesslike purposes usually had cases of solid oak. Even oak was veneered however, if of the wavy grained pollard variety. Small country makers made one-hand clocks with seconds pendulums that ran for thirty hours in simple oak cases or white wood cases with a painted 'grain' throughout the period of the long case. They are often taken for clocks made very much earlier because of the single hand.

The longcase clock was by far the most accurate clock of its time and its timekeeping was responsible for detecting the fact that days measured by the transits of the sun vary in length throughout the year. A clock is about sixteen minutes fast of the sundial at one time of the year and fourteen minutes slow of it at another. As a sundial

was used to set a clock to time, it was necessary to know the difference, called 'the equation of time'. Good clocks were therefore provided with printed tables showing these figures and a few showed the equation of time automatically by a separate hand on the dial.

Longcase clocks were commonly made with dials giving the day of the month, valuable information when newspapers were uncommon. Many had moon dials because it was useful to know when the moon would provide enough light at night in days when there were no street lamps and torches. It became known among English clockmakers in the 18th century that times of the tides are associated with phases of the moon. Not infrequently the moon dial also indicated times of local high tides, for use of fishermen and the many who used boats for travel.

Makers of better clocks supplied sundials and equatio of time tables with them so that they could be set t time and their timekeeping checked.

Bracket clocks with spring drive and short pendulum were made in large numbers by London makers fro about 1660 to well after 1800. Similar bracket clock were also produced by the French, the Dutch, and th Austrians. Cases were made of wood, usually ebony venee or imitation ebony, but sometimes in walnut or anothe wood. Later ones were sometimes in mahogany and ver late ones in oak. The size was usually fairly large b modern standards, about fifteen inches or so high. Som of the top quality bracket clocks by London maker were much smaller, however.

Movements of the clocks were spring-driven throug

a fusee, but they retained the verge escapement with a short pendulum, about ten inches long, for many years after the much better anchor had been in use with long-case clocks. The reason was probably that the verge was less sensitive to the clock's being level.

In 1676, a parson clockmaker, the Rev. Edward Barlow, invented rack striking that prevented the hands from becoming out of phase with the striking. Its extra value at the time was that it made repeating clocks and watches possible.

English bracket clocks often have repeater mechanisms. There is a cord from one side of the clock (or from both sides in better clocks) which, when pulled, causes the clock to sound the last hour on a bell. Some repeaters sound the quarter hour, half hour, or three-quarters as well. Repeater clocks went out of fashion after the safety match was invented in the first quarter of the 19th century.

Some makers specialised in clocks for export, particularly to the Turkish market. They included Markwick Markham, Christopher Gould, and James Cox. Often these were musical clocks. Cox, who was really an *entrepreneur*, specialised in elaborate clocks with automata, including waterfalls in which flowing water was imitated by rotating rods of twisted glass, and moving animals.

Eventually several firms sprang up making both bracket and longcase clock movements and supplying them to the 'makers' so that the name on the dial of many clocks from the second half of the 18th century and right through the 19th are often of the workmaster assembler or the retailer. One of these early manufacturing firms, Thwaites and Reed, is still in existence in Clerkenwell, and now making tower clocks. They supplied many very eminent makers, with not only movements but with complete clocks. This is known from their 18th century records, now lodged in the Guildhall.

In the second half of the 18th century, large clocks were made for inns and taverns. The tavern clock was weight-driven and had a long pendulum like a grandfather clock, but hung on the wall. Its most notable feature was the huge dial, two or three feet across, made of wood and without glass. A tax was imposed on clocks and watches from 1797 to 1798 and so many people gave up using them and began relying on the tavern clock, that tavern clocks acquired a new name, 'Act of Parliament clocks'.

In the short time of the tax it almost destroyed the manufacturing industry.

Special large clock-watches were made from the later 17th century to be hung in coaches. From the later 18th century, many small 'sedan clocks' were made. They were watch movements in round wooden frames.

From about 1750, bracket clocks began to appear with a round instead of the traditional square dial. Balloon clocks, based on a typical French bracket clock shape with a waist and rounded top, came into fashion. They earned their name later in the 18th century when Mongolfier introduced his hot air rigid balloons of similar outline. Other domestic clocks with wooden cases introduced after 1800 were the lancet, with a Gothic shaped top, and the chamfer top, both generally called 'Regency

LEFT: *Japanese pillar clock*
A pointer on the weight
indicates the hour

RIGHT: *Dial of a night clo*
made by Petrus Campanus
in 1683

Both clocks are in the
BRITISH MUSEUM

TOP LEFT: Picture clock of the Southern German baroque period, c. 1730. The subject is Vanitas, painted in oils on wood. The clock shows the time, date, and signs of the zodiac WUPPERTALER UHRENMUSEUM, W. GERMANY

ABOVE: French ormulu and white marble pillar clock of the early 19th century BIGGS OF MAIDENHEAD

LEFT: Carriage clock by Oudin of Paris that repeats the quarter hours on gongs and also has an alarm and a calendar BIGGS OF MAIDENHEAD

cks' today. The name is also used for the many styles
French clock copied by English makers.

About the same time, another English clock became
ry well known as the 'English dial', because it hung
the wall and appeared to be nothing more than a
rge circular dial with white face and, usually, blued
eel hands. The movement was behind the dial, spring-
iven with a pendulum. It was used in kitchens and
fices and by public services. A variation was the 'drop
al' which has a little box below the dial to accommodate
e pendulum.

Another clock of the Victorian period had a skeleton
ame, so that all the wheels could be seen, mounted on a
ooden or marble base and covered by a glass shade or
me. The French were first to produce these, as early
1750. In a way, the style was a reversion to the 16th-
ntury Gothic clock. English makers took up the skeleton
ock very enthusiastically, when the clocks became very
opular, after a French skeleton clock was shown at the
reat Exhibition of 1851 in London.

Industrial clocks have an earlier history than most
eople imagine. The first were invented by John White-
urst of Derby in 1750. He made watchman's clocks in
ng cases. A turning dial had pegs around its edge.
he watchman has to operate a lever or punch on the
de of the clock when he visits it which leaves a record
n the dial until cancelled. Black Forest makers in Ger-
any copied the idea. In 1868, Dr. Thurgar of Norwich,
vented a clock that would turn gas street lamps on
d off automatically and a Bournemouth builder, John
unning, first used them. Later versions adjusted them-
elves automatically to suit the hours of darkness. Electric
me switches followed.

The assault on the British market by cheaper American
ocks and then by cheaper German ones gradually
estroyed the British industry which concentrated on
eavier fusee clocks with filed-out steel parts, while the
mericans and Germans used thin rolled brass and bent
ire. Only one company with a substantial output
anaged to compete. It was S. Smith and Sons, which
tarted as a small watchmakers shop in The Strand,
ondon, and is now Smiths Industries Clock and Watch
Division, which has the most modern alarm clock factory
Europe and is the only English maker of jewelled lever
atches.

The German clock industry in Augsburg and Nurem-
erg did not outlast the 17th century and a new one
rew up in the Black Forest area, which is also in the
outhern part of the country. Early clockmakers there
ere woodworkers and farmers who, towards the end of
he 17th century, developed clocks to suit their own
aw materials and skills. Almost every part of the early
lack Forest clock was made of wood, including all the
oothed wheels, and bells were made of glass. The escape-
ent was the verge with a foliot. Farmer-clockmakers

also sold their own clocks, carting them around in special
packs on their backs.

The pendulum was introduced into the Black Forest
some time after 1750 and was hung in front of the dial
and combined with a verge escapement. The dial itself
was painted on wood and there was no glass. The clock
hung on the wall with its weights suspended below.
Locally, clocks with the pendulum in front of the dial
were called 'cow's tails'.

Black Forest makers produced many novelties. Their
picture clocks were like framed paintings that hung on
the wall, but the clock in the tower in the painting was
a real one. Some had animated scenes showing wind-

French lyre clock of about 1800 in a bronze case set with
onyx HAGANS CLOCK MANOR MUSEUM, COLORADO

mills working, people sawing wood, children on see saws, musicians, performing animals, and other event The construction was of wood, paper and wire and almo always highly ingenious.

In 1740, Franz Ketterer invented a novelty clock i which a cuckoo appeared to herald the hour. This becam the most famous Black Forest clock of all. Early ones ha a flat rectangular painted dial. Much later the clock cas was made to look like a wooden mountain chalet, whic probably accounts for the common delusion that they ar Swiss.

Musical clocks were made in some numbers as well a dial clocks, 'postman's alarms' (a cheap wooden alarr with two bells on top and often without a glass), and later on, four-hundred-day or anniversary clocks, whicl run under glass domes for a year slow with beating tor sion pendulums below the movements.

The Black Forest industry was nearly ruined by Ameri can machine-made clocks, but underwent a miraculou recovery after 1851, when Erhard Junghans managed t persuade it to adopt modern production methods. Today it is the world's most prolific clock industry in botl production and commercial ideas. Inventions of recen years include a balance wheel suspended on a magneti field so that it is practically frictionless, various forms o battery-driven clock that are quickly becoming more pop ular than handwound clocks, and a clock that is self winding because daylight or artificial light falling on solar cell recharges its driving batteries.

Most recent of the battery clocks, the Diehl Dilectrion represents a big step in very accurate timekeeping at low

cost. It follows the principle of the free pendulum described in Chapter 8. Instead of a free pendulum and a slave pendulum, however, there is a free balance wheel and a tiny slave synchronous motor. The balance is kept swinging by a battery and transistorised circuit, and it does no work. The battery also drives the little synchronous motor that turns the hands. The ingenious part is an electronic link between the balance and the motor which enables tiny pulses of current from the balance to control the rate at which the motor turns.

The French clock industry was one of the earliest, if not the earliest, and good craftsmanship and clever design was evident from the earliest times. Louis XIV, the 'Sun King', who reigned from 1643 to 1714, went out of his way to attract to the court not only French but foreign clock and watchmakers. French clocks of this time were highly ornamented with acanthus leaves and draperies made in gilded metal called 'ormolu'. It was the time when elaborate inlay work called 'boule' or 'buhl' with brass or pewter set in tortoiseshell appeared.

During the following years, French clocks changed recognisably in style and were almost always ornate compared with English and other countries' productions. Nevertheless, French makers were technically active too, and were responsible for a number of successful escapement inventions.

A-L. Breguet, of Paris, made clocks in the 18th century embodying the first principle of industrial automation, only rediscovered in this century. Breguet called this kind of clock 'pendule sympathique'. It was designed for use with special pocket watches. Before retiring, the owner places his watch in a holder in the top of the clock. During the night, the clock not only sets the watch to time and winds it, *but also adjusts its regulator to correct its timekeeping error.* It employs the principle known in automation as 'feedback'.

Breguet was responsible for the later popularity of the French carriage clock. For his officers, Napoleon wanted special travelling clocks, which became known as 'pendules d'officieur'. Breguet made them in small brass and glass cases with handles on top. They developed into the brass case with all glass sides called a 'pendule de voyage', or carriage clock, and its manufacture became separate industries in St Nicholas d'Aliermont, near Dieppe, and at Besançon, near the Swiss border, the present French watchmaking centre, and elsewhere.

The French went furthest in the 19th century with rationalising their clock industry because they turned out movements in brass drums of more or less standard sizes so that the makers of the elaborate cases could just buy movements complete and fit them without trouble.

During the Industrial Revolution, and up to the First World War, the French industry developed a large export

ABOVE: Dutch bracket clock of about 1675 by Johannes van Ceulen, with spring drive and pendulum. The dial is velvet covered. The first pendulum clock was similar in type

TOP LEFT: All wooden Black Forest, Germany, clock with half-hour striking and alarm. The two bells are of glass and a figure pulls a cord to strike them. This kind of clock is often wrongly called a 'Dutch clock'

LEFT: Clockmaker clock of about 1790, made in Vienna, Austria, or the Black Forest of Germany, with a thirty-hour verge movement. This is how they peddled their clocks RALPH COX, LINCOLN

market for novelty clocks expressing the spirit of the time. The clocks imitated steam engines, beam engines, lighthouses, submarines, and ticket machines, and there were mystery clocks of several kinds. One mystery clock has hands apparently suspended in mid air. Another has a figure holding a pendulum from an outstretched arm. There is no apparent connection between the pendulum and the clock and the figure appears stationary, yet the pendulum swings of its own accord and controls the rate of the clock.

France had many regional clockmaking industries, their most typical product being a wall or longcase clock with an extremely wide and elaborately embossed and coloured pendulum.

French mantel clocks were so numerous in style it is impossible to describe them in detail. They incorporated almost every conceivable kind of figure, event, building, ornament.

The Dutch made clocks from a fairly early date, but missed their chance of developing the pendulum clock, although it was invented by a Dutchman. Dutch makers adopted the pendulum but clung to the older form of posted frame movement of the lantern clock. They made ornate wall clocks, a hooded wall clock with a long

ABOVE: Italian picture clock of the early 18th century, which [is] also a night clock. The Star of Bethlehem shows the [h]our, illuminated from behind by a candle
WUPPERTALER UHRENMUSEUM, W. GERMANY

TOP RIGHT: Steam engine clock made during the Industrial Revolution in Belfast. It won a prize at the Paris Exhibition [of] 1889 ULSTER MUSEUM, NORTHERN IRELAND

RIGHT: Movement of a talking clock made in 1914. The clock [se]ts off a gramophone motor which plays from a recorded loop
WUPPERTALER UHRENMUSEUM, W. GERMANY

[p]endulum enclosed in a very shallow trunk, and long-[c]ase clocks very much like the English ones but with [b]ulbous bases.

The Dutch still get the credit for many Black Forest [c]locks, especially those with animated wooden figures [a]bove the dial, because in the past 'Deutsch' was mistaken [f]or 'Dutch'.

The Austrians were also very active clockmakers pro-[d]ucing bracket clocks, clocks similar to Black Forest [p]roducts, and some particularly fine carriage clocks. Two [t]ypes were exclusive: the 'zappler', a miniature clock with [a] fast wagging pendulum hanging in front, and the [V]ienna regulator, a wall clock with long pendulum and [g]lass front to the case. A peculiarity of the later and [c]heaper Vienna regulators is that the seconds hand goes [r]ound the sixty divisions in forty-five seconds!

As it isolated itself from the rest of the world, Japan [h]ad a system of temporal hours until as late as 1873. [C]locks still had verge escapements, but with two foliots, [o]ne for night hours and one for day hours. They could [t]herefore be set to run at one rate during the day and [a]nother at night. Hour divisions on the dials were adjust-[a]ble or dials replaceable. Japanese clocks are therefore a [s]tudy in themselves.

Navigating by time

When a ship is on the open sea, there are no landmarks to guide it. After the 15th century, when Portuguese navigators began to make long ocean voyages, to be utterly lost was a common experience of most sailors. The navigator who ventured away from the coast had to be something of an astronomer and mathematician to find his position north or south (his latitude) by taking an observation of the height of the sun in day-time, or of certain stars at night. To find his position east or west (his longitude) was almost impossible. Because the earth spins on its axis, it upsets astronomical calculations.

As there was no satisfactory way of calculating the ship's position, east and west, a captain would sail a compass course – sail by 'dead reckoning' – but after a few weeks he would almost certainly be carried perhaps hundreds of miles off course by unknown currents.

This was the cause of a great disaster in 1701 when the Mediterranean Fleet, running before a westerly gale with sails reefed, found itself suddenly and at night amongst the rocks of the Isles of Scilly. Caught like this, the men-o-war were helpless. Four went to the bottom and the commander in chief and hundreds of men were drowned.

Some years previously, the Royal Observatory ha been set up at Greenwich to discover an astronomic solution to the problem, but so many ships were bein lost with their crews and cargoes that, in 1714, th British Government passed an Act of Parliament offerin prizes for practical methods of finding the longitude a sea. The top award was £ 20,000 – worth over £ 100,00 ($ 280,000) today – for determining longitude on boar a ship to within half a degree.

The charts of the time were not accurate for simila reasons. It was not in fact until the 17th century tha the lengths of a degree of latitude and longitude wer measured with any degree of accuracy.

Other countries too had been finding the problem s serious a handicap to trade, that King Philip III of Spai had offered a prize long before the British, in 1598. Th Dutch, the Venetians, and the French also tried to en courage an invention in the same way, but the Britis

ABOVE: John Harrison, who made the first successful sea clock

RIGHT: John Harrison's first sea clock, known as H1
NATIONAL MARITIME MUSEUM, GREENWICH

prize was the only one ever paid and the story of the struggle for it is one of the most fascinating in any field of endeavour.

The Act of 1714 caused the same kind of surge of scientific effort that space research does today, and was in many ways responsible for the Industrial Revolution that followed. The invention of the marine chronometer for which it was directly responsible, resulted eventually in the domination of the world by the British Fleet, the expansion of trading, and the acquisition of the British Empire.

Instruments for a ship's navigator at the time were a sand glass and log line with chip to measure the ship's speed, a compass for setting a course and a quadrant or sextant for finding local time.

In 1530, a Flemish mathematician, Gemma Frisius, suggested that an accurate clock on a ship would enable longitude to be calculated. If this showed time at the port from which the ship sailed, it could be compared with local time obtained by observation of the sun; the difference would give the longitude of the ship, since four minutes of time is equal to one degree of longitude.

The Dutch scientist, Christiaan Huygens, was the first to try (unsuccessfully) to devise a clock that would run accurately on board a rolling and pitching ship. The accurate clocks of the time were those driven by weight and controlled by the pendulum method that Huygens had invented, but while a spring drive could be used, a pendulum would not work, however gentle the motion of the ship. Mathematicians, astronomers, and clock makers of the time all strove for solutions.

Eventually two main possibilities emerged. One was the marine timekeeper, the other an astronomical method based on lunar distances, called 'lunars'. Using lunars meant finding the position of the moon in relation to the sun and stars to give the local longitude.

But it was not a scientist or clockmaker in the ordinary sense who solved the problem of the longitude. It was a man who was brought up as a carpenter in the Lincolnshire village of Barrow, near the River Humber. He had no formal schooling and served no apprenticeship in clockmaking. His name was John Harrison. He and his younger brother James at an early age started a sideline repairing clocks. Before John was twenty, in 1713, the brothers had made at least one wonderful clock almost entirely of wood. Part of it is today in the Museum of the Worshipful Company of Clockmakers in London.

TOP LEFT: John Harrison's second timekeeper, H2, which is inscribed 'Made for His Majesty George the IInd. By order of a Committee Held the 30th of June 1737'
NATIONAL MARITIME MUSEUM, GREENWICH

LEFT: John Harrison's third marine timekeeper, H3
NATIONAL MARITIME MUSEUM, GREENWICH

John Harrison was probably the designer and James the maker.

News of the £20,000 would have been sensational in the busy port of Hull near their village. The brothers at this time were concentrating on making more and more accurate longcase clocks. The clocks showed remarkable technical advances without drawing on orthodox ideas. For example, the clocks had wooden wheels and bearings as anti-friction devices needing no oil, and were ingeniously compensated against the effects of changing temperature.

By 1726, the two brothers had one and probably two clocks that would keep time, John Harrison recorded, without the variation of more than a single second in a month'. The clocks were without doubt the most accurate in the world at the time – yet designed and made by two young carpenters in an isolated country village away from any clockmaking centre.

Almost as startling were the methods they had to adopt to measure the accuracy of the clocks. First, John Harrison had to draw up extra accurate tables of the equation of time so that the clocks could be checked more accurately against the sun, but this was still not good enough, so he employed star time, the sidereal time of the astronomers.

Certain clock stars pass the same point three minutes fifty-six seconds earlier on successive nights. By eye, John Harrison aligned the edge of one of his window frames with a neighbour's chimney about twenty-five yards away and also with a clock star, so that he could note the exact instant when the clock star disappeared behind the chimney. A helper called out the seconds shown by the clock, so that Harrison would know the time shown by the clock when the star disappeared. If the star disappeared exactly three minutes fifty-six seconds earlier the next night, the clock was exactly on time.

It was while the brothers were making these longcase precision clocks that they determined to design a 'sea clock' on the same principles, but spring-driven and with a balance instead of pendulum.

One of their biggest problems was the unsuitability of wood for the sea clock. For the main parts they would have to use brass, which was expensive. They knew, however, that the Act of Parliament permitted the Board of Longitude to advance money to assist inventors. So it was decided that John should go to London to apply to the Commissioners.

He managed to obtain an interview with Dr. Halley, who was the Astronomer Royal as well as a member of the Board of Longitude which had been appointed to deal with applicants for the prizes offered under the Act. Halley was impressed, but wanted the opinion of a clockmaker, so sent Harrison to see George Graham, in Fleet Street, who was an eminent scientific instrument maker and a Fellow of the Royal Society, as well as

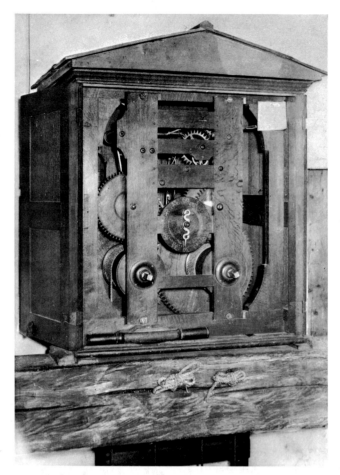

Wooden clock by James Harrison at Brocklesbury Park
BRITISH HOROLOGICAL INSTITUTE, NOTTINGHAM
BRANCH ANTIQUARIAN GROUP

being a clockmaker. At this point a trait in Harrison's character, his distrust of outsiders, make him protest against the proposal in case Graham stole his ideas. Halley assured him of Graham's integrity and also hinted that Harrison would have to be more tactful, having apparently decided that despite his originality, Harrison was somewhat boastful and talkative.

The advice was not taken, for Harrison later recorded: 'Mr. Graham began as I thought very roughly with me, and the which had like to have occasioned me to become rough too; but however we got the ice broke...' Graham became interested in Harrison's drawings and they talked from about ten in the morning until eight at night. Graham encouraged Harrison to go back to Barrow and build his sea clock on condition that, if it turned out well, he and Dr. Halley would back Harrison in an approach to the Board for money to develop it.

Harrison agreed and, because this did not solve the immediate financial problem, Graham generously lent some money free of interest. The East India Company, which was very concerned to reduce shipping losses, and several private individuals also provided gifts of money and loans during the five years it took to build the first

Experimental watch made by John Jeffreys to John Harrison's design to try out ideas for the large sea watch, H4
NATIONAL MARITIME MUSEUM, GREENWICH

The large watch, H4 which eventually won the £20,000 prize for John Harrison NATIONAL MARITIME MUSEUM, GREENWICH

sea clock, a heavy machine measuring over three feet in each direction.

This clock, now known as 'H1', was tested on board a barge on the Humber and adjusted to give a satisfactory performance, so the brothers decided to approach the Board of Longitude. It turned out the Board had never met! But the Royal Society examined H1, approved of it (except for its size) and arranged to test it on board ship from Portsmouth to Lisbon and back. John Harrison made the big decision to go with it.

On the way back, Harrison's prediction of the ship's position was sixty miles more accurate than the captain's. When the Board met afterwards to hear Harrison's report, Harrison was less self-opinionated than usual and said he would prefer to make another, smaller, sea clock, rather than modify the first to increase its accuracy. He asked for £500 outright to make the new clock over two years. The Board agreed, but imposed some tough conditions including the giving of both H1 (which they had not paid for) and the proposed H2 to the nation.

An interesting fact that appeared later was that H1 would have won a longitude prize if corrections for rate had been applied. At the time it was thought that a precision clock must keep exact time of day; it was subsequently discovered that the most accurate rate of a clock or watch is not necessarily time of day. For example, if a clock gains *exactly* one second a day, its rate is perfect. To obtain time of day it is only necessary to subtract one second for every day that passes. If H1 had been corrected in this way, it would have been correct to about three seconds a day.

Both brothers worked on H2, but it was never given a test at sea, either because of the war with Spain or because John was pessimistic about it, despite the fact that it incorporated a big improvement, a spring remontoire which got rid of any variations of power in the spring drive. There may have been another reason. It seems the brothers split up at this time so there was probably a dispute between them. James gave up making sea clocks and turned to milling, bell founding, and astrology.

John, in the meantime, had been working on his own on a third sea clock. He experimented no further with H2, and in 1741 told the Board about H3 and asked for another £500 on the promise that H3 would be ready in two years for a trial to the West Indies.

His estimate was somewhat optimistic. It took nineteen years for H3 to be finished and adjusted for its test! It incorporated a bi-metallic strip which bent according to the temperature and lengthened or shortened the balance spring to compensate for the effects of temperature changes. This invention turned out to be of the utmost benefit to man, because it was the thermostat used today in millions of devices including kitchen ovens and flashing direction indicators.

During these nineteen years, Harrison and his family lived in great poverty because he was so engrossed in his sea clock that he had no time to earn enough to support them. The Royal Society helped him financially from time to time and also awarded him their highest honour, the Copley gold medal. The Board granted him another £500.

Harrison's last timekeeper, H5, made in 1770. It was tested in King George III's private observatory

Simplified version of Harrison's H4 made by Larcum Kendall in 1771 and issued to Captain Bligh of 'The Bounty'. It is known as K2

When Harrison wrote to the Board in 1755 to tell them he expected to have H3 ready for its sea trial in 1756, he told them he was also making two watches, one for the pocket and the other much larger. The smaller watch was made to Harrison's design by a John Jefferys to try out certain ideas. It was not known to be still in existence until a few years ago when it was discovered by Colonel H. Quill, past Master of the Worshipful Company of Clockmakers. It had suffered in a bombing raid during the Second World War, but was restored and is in the Museum of the Worshipful Company of Clockmakers.

John Harrison still did not have H3 ready by 1757, and had again to appeal to the Board, but now the Board was wary and told him to keep H3 for another year for adjustment, but to have one of the watches ready for testing at sea. Harrison was so impoverished by now that he was trying to win a prize of £50 for designing a cheap corn mill. The Board, however, provided another grant, making his total £3000 over twenty-seven years.

It was in fact three years later, in 1760, that Harrison announced that H3 was ready. At the same time he produced the large sea watch for the Board to see, remarking that it would be a sea timekeeper in its own right, not just an ancillary to the sea clock as he had first proposed. The sea watch must have impressed the Board, because they allowed Harrison a year to adjust it and granted him another £500.

The watch, now called H4, turned out to be the most famous watch ever made and ever likely to be made. Although designed by John Harrison, the construct-

ion was probably by John Jefferys, Larcum Kendall, and perhaps John Harrison's son, William, who was then twenty-seven, but had shown no great desire to be a clockmaker. The watch is in a silver case about 5¼ inches in diameter and eventually took fifteen years to make.

When at last John Harrison had a timekeeper, this large watch, that he considered ready for testing at sea he was *sixty-seven years old*, and had spent his whole life trying to make his timekeepers more and more accurate.

It was decided that William Harrison should accompany H4 on a voyage from Portsmouth to Jamaica. Astronomers would determine the local times at Plymouth and Port Royal in Jamaica to compare the times shown by the watch.

John Harrison immediately objected to the method proposed for calculating the longitude in Jamaica, as he said it could lead to an error of thirty miles. The Board apparently agreed.

At last on 18th November, 1761 the square rigger *H.M.S. Deptford* set sail in bad weather from Portsmouth with the watch resting on a cushion in Captain Digges' cabin, and with William Harrison and an astronomer on board. Ten days out, the captain was not certain whether he was east or west of Madeira, although the navigator had estimated the ship's position by dead reckoning. William Harrison was able to calculate that Madeira was still nearly a hundred miles to the west, and also give the time at which they would sight another island. This information was correct and profoundly impressed the ship's company, especially as they were then able to pick up some butts of wine in Madeira. The Master recorded

in his log a few days earlier: 'This day all Beer was expended, the People obliged to drink water.'

At last they arrived in Jamaica and Harrison must have been on tenterhooks while the astronomer set up his instruments. To win the £20,000 prize, the watch had to be not more than one minute fifty-four seconds out after eighty-one days and a rough sea passage in extremes of temperature.

William Harrison returned rather precipitously, perhaps because of the war with Spain, and reported that the passage was so bad, the watch was thrown around the cabin by the bucking of the ship. He and his father did a calculation which showed that H4 had lost only 5.1 seconds during the voyage, well within the limits required by the Act. This was arrived at by calculating the losing rate as 2.66 seconds a day. It was equivalent to an error of only one and a quarter miles, an incredibly good result.

The prize was theirs, or so they thought. The Board thought otherwise; they made three objections, that the astronomical observations at Plymouth were inaccurate, that insufficient observations were made in Jamaica, and that the rules of the Royal Society had not been followed (which was quite untrue). John Harrison replied in detail.

The Board met again and decided that, 'the Experiments already made of the Watch have not been sufficient to determine the Longitude at Sea.' The reason for this decision was probably that they misunderstood the correction for rate. But even without correction for rate, H4 would have won a prize of £10,000 under the Act.

Harrison seems to have waited in frustration and the following year the Board decided there should be another trial to the West Indies. Harrison was forced to agree. The Board advanced him £2,500 to be repaid from any prize he won.

This marked a turning point in Harrison's dealings with the Board, which he had trusted all these years. His animosity was most strongly directed at the members who supported the lunar method of finding the longitude for which there was a strong scientific following. He set up what would now be called a 'public relations operation' to express his grievances in public, by persuading literary friends to help him write pamphlets addressed to the public and Members of Parliament.

*TOP LEFT: Marine chronometer by John Arnold,
now belonging to the Royal Society*

*LEFT: Regulator clock in a sealed case made for Armagh Observatory
Northern Ireland by Thomas Earnshaw, who, on receiving
the order, remarked that he had never made a clock and did not
even know how many wheels were in one. But he made a fine
regulator and later two others, one of which is in the USA*
DR. LINDSAY, ASTRONOMER ROYAL, AND MR. JOHN RIDDELL,
ARMAGH, NORTHERN IRELAND

Both the Board and some of his own friends encouraged him to disclose the details of the mechanism of H4 before the second trial, in case H4 was lost at sea. After resistance, Harrison agreed. The French Governement sent an unsuccessful commission to London to try to learn the secrets of H4. Harrison was now seventy years of age, and had given his son the duty of dealing with the Board.

John Harrison next turned to the offensive. He had a change of heart and tried to prevent H4 from being taken to sea again. He petitioned Parliament for a new Act which would make the award due to him, and give legal protection against copying when he disclosed his inventions. One of the supporters of the petition was the King himself, George III. Parliament acted swiftly and passed an Act giving Harrison the protection he needed, but making him an award of only £5,000, to be deducted from any prize he might win.

Members of the Board immediately interpreted the Act in their own way, telling Harrison that they wanted not only drawings and descriptions, of H4, *but two exact copies of the watch* made under his supervision, and that these duplicate watches should be tested to convince the Board whether other workmen could make them too. This was extremely harsh. It would mean years before Harrison could claim the prize money to which he was entitled.

One of the men to take astronomical measurements on the new test was the Rev. Nevil Maskelyne, who had worked out such an effective method of using lunars, although the calculations were long and complicated, that the Board had backed the publication of some tables.

This did not suit Harrison. He was suspicious of Maskelyne from the start and became more and more so in the following years until he had an obsession with all 'Priests and Professors'. Because Maskelyne was in poor health, it was decided that the trial this time should be to the Barbados. He departed ahead of William Harrison.

William, setting sail on 28th March, 1764 from Spithead, repeated his accurate reckoning of the ship's position and forecasts of landfalls, with the aid of H4. When he arrived in Barbados, he found Maskelyne had been talking about his rival lunar method and at once decided that Maskelyne was a 'most improper person' to test H4. After a dispute, the observations were carried out.

After the return of William Harrison and Maskelyne, four mathematicians were appointed to work out the results independently. The Board met to hear their conclusions, but did not invite John Harrison. The average of the four independent calculations showed an error of 39.2 seconds, equivalent to 9.8 miles – three times more accurate than that required to win the top prize of £20,000.

At last, the Harrisons thought, at last after thirty-four years of extreme effort, the prize would without any doubt be handed over. They thought in vain.

At the next meeting of the Board, which included the Rev. Nevil Maskelyne, who had just been appointed Astronomer Royal, Lord Morton pointed out that Harrison had not yet disclosed the secrets of H4. The Board therefore concluded that they could not decide how practical and useful H4 was at sea until the operation and construction had been disclosed. When Harrison did this, they said, he would be paid £10,000, less the advance of £2,500 he had received. The remainder would only be paid when he proved that the construction would provide a 'Method of Common and general Utility'.

Harrison, now aged seventy-two, was incensed and issued a stream of pamphlets and broadsheets. The Board was silent. Maskelyne had proved to them that he had

Modern chronometer for surveyors, made by Thomas Mercer of St. Albans, England

predicted the latitude of Barbados by lunars to within thirty miles and the Isle of Wight to within ten miles. They probably thought this the more practical way of finding the longitude.

The Board arranged for their decisions to be incorporated in a new Act. Harrison petitioned Parliament against it, but this time without success. He was required to give details of his machines within six months and to surrender all four machines as soon as he had received the first part of the prize.

Anyone else but the dogged ex-carpenter from Yorkshire would probably have given in at this stage, faced with the authority of Parliament and the success of lunars, and especially the instruction to construct two duplicate timekeepers at his age. Harrison was called to a series of meetings with the Board. He took William with him as a spokesman who explained that his father would hand over drawings and explanations in writing. The Board thought John Harrison would be evasive, and laid down strict conditions. Eventually Harrison walked out declaring he would not comply with the demands, 'so long as he had a drop of English blood in his body.'

William Harrison was asked to help and refused. There was deadlock and eventually John Harrison had to write to the Board to apologise.

At the next meeting, John Harrison was required to sign an oath that he would comply with the requirements. William refused, saying his father did not understand it and the chairman, Lord Egmont, exclaimed heatedly 'Sir, I have told you that we will not hear you talk, for you are the strangest and most obstinate creature that I have ever met with and, would you do what we want you to do, and which is in your power, I will give you my word to give you the money, if you will but do it'.

And at last John and William Harrison signed the oath and deposited descriptions and drawings of the timekeeper. A committee of six spent six days at Harrison's house in Red Lion Square in London, where he had moved some years previously, hearing explanations of the mechanism.

The Board authorised the payment making up the first £10,000 as soon as he had handed over the four timekeepers, but Harrison pleaded to keep H4 to help in the construction of the two duplicates. The Board refused. They did however authorise him to collect the sum of £7,500.

For the remaining £10,000 he still had to produce the two duplicates, although he had surrendered both his original drawings and the watch. Harrison suggested he should engage craftsmen to make two duplicates of H4 for the nation, but the Board turned down the scheme. Instead they decided to give H4 a ten months' trial at the Royal Observatory under the Rev. Nevil Maskelyne and to compare the results with those of H1, H2, and H3. This was the sting in the tail, for Harrison still held the first three sea clocks.

The Rev. Nevil Maskelyne called on Harrison unexpectedly at Red Lion Square armed with a letter of authority from the Board requiring the timekeepers to be handed over. There was a quarrel and Harrison stumped upstairs. Afterwards he declared the three machines had been damaged on removal.

Maskelyne published the results of his test, which were not very favourable because he did not correct for rate. Harrison was furious and issued another pamphlet putting his objections. Next the Board loaned H4 to Larcum Kendall to make a duplicate, which he completed in 1770, two years later. His watch, called K1, was so beautifully made that even William Harrison was compelled to admit that in some ways it was superior to his father's. Kendall told the Board, however, that he could not agree to their plan to control the making of a number of similar watches because the adjusting raised too many problems.

Larcum Kendall was so quick in comparison with Harrison that the Board began to put the pressure on Harrison, demanding the two duplicate watches within five years (when he would be eighty-two) or forfeit the £10,000 owing. They also proposed to send K1, two timekeepers by John Arnold, and Harrison's new H5, on a test with Captain Cook, who was preparing for his second voyage of discovery in the Pacific Ocean. But H5 was not ready. When it was, Harrison was seventy-nine. He was ill and his sight failing. The chances of his making the second duplicate required by the Board were negligible. He decided to approach King George III to have the watch tested in the King's private observatory in Richmond Park, Surrey. He approached the King's Swiss astronomer who arranged for an audience. After hearing

e full story from John Harrison and his son (who was
essed in a lace suit for the occasion and, it is recorded,
as taken by the Royal children for a nobleman), the
ing exclaimed: 'These people have been cruelly treated.
y God, Harrison, I will see you righted!'

Unfortunately the test of H5 had an almost fatal start.
behaved extremely erratically. Then the King remem-
ered he had left some powerful lodestones (natural mag-
ts) in a drawer nearby. Later the watch was found to
ave a very good rate. Harrison again appealed to the
oard, but was once more turned down despite the King's
upport. He then approached Lord North, the Prime
Minister, asking for 'bare justice'. Lord North was not
esponsive so Harrison circulated a pamphlet to every
Member of Parliament and presented a petition to the
House.

The petition was debated in Parliament in 1772 but
o conclusion was reached and Harrison withdrew it to
ffer a new one, apparently on advice. The new one
erely asked for a special award, pointing out that Harri-
on had spent his life working on his sea clocks and was
oo old to comply with the remaining conditions.

On 21st June, 1773, Parliament agreed to pay Harri-
on £8,760 over what he had already received. This
rought the total to £18,750, plus the grants over the
ears which totalled £4,000.

The Harrisons were not very grateful. It is clear
ey hated becoming supplicants for what they considered
heir rights. William Harrison remarked that they had
een 'stung out of £1,250'. His father's comment was,
s I do not now mind the money, the Devil may take the
riests' – a reference to the Rev. Nevil Maskelyne.

John Harrison remained sour to the last, but was still
orking on a precision clock when he died in 1776 at
he age of eighty-three. He is buried in Hampstead
hurchyard.

K1, Kendall's copy of H4, proved to be amazingly
ccurate and enabled Captain Cook to plot the first, and
xceptionally precise, charts of New Zealand and Austra-
sia. Kendall made two cheaper versions, now known
s K2 and K3, by eliminating the complications, but this
lso eliminated the extreme accuracy. K1 was issued to
Captain Bligh when he sailed in *The Bounty*, a floating
onservatory that was to collect breadfruit plants from
ahiti to be replanted in the West Indies.

When some of the crew mutinied under Fletcher
Christian, Captain Bligh and eighteen others were set
drift in the ship's launch, and Bligh performed an
mazing feat of navigation in the open boat over nearly
our thousand miles. The watch was taken by Christian
o Pitcairn Island, where some mutineers settled. Sixteen
ears after some of the mutineers had been found in
ahiti and three had been hanged from the yard-arm of a
hip in Portsmouth harbour, Captain Mayhew Folger of
he American sealer *Topaz* found an unnamed island and

*Marine chronometer made in 1796 by Ferdinand Berthoud,
who won a prize of the French Royal Academy of Science
and became sole supplier to the French Navy*

was amazed to hear children shouting at him in English.
Their father was Alexander Smith, one of the mutineers,
who gave Folger the timepiece, K1, and an azimouth
compass from *The Bounty*. The other mutineers were
dead, having murdered each other or been killed by the
natives.

Later the watch was stolen from Folger and turned up
in Concepción, in Chile, when bought by an old Spanish
muleteer. Eventually it was bought in Valparaiso by a
Royal Navy captain, and brought to England in 1843.

Thomas Mudge, one of those appointed to examine
Harrison's No. 4 watch, became so obsessed also with the

problem of sea clocks that he more or less abandoned his flourishing business of making high quality clocks and watches. Despite the magnificent workmanship of Mudge's main machines, called the 'Blue' and the 'Green' after the colours of their cases, both failed on trials at Greenwich. Mudge and his son had a dispute with the Board, like the Harrisons, and eventually obtained £2,500 from Parliament, to the Board's chagrin.

In France, parallel work on sea clocks was going on, principally by Pierre Le Roy, clockmaker to the King, and Ferdinand Berthoud, who was horologist to the French Ministry of Marine. Le Roy spent twenty years and a large part of his fortune on the problem and received a small amount of prize money and a medal from the French government as a reward. His real achievement was to detach the balance wheel so that it swung with a minimum of interference.

Le Roy went to first principles and he must be credited with designing the true forerunner of the modern ship's chronometer. Harrison, as Lt. Commander Gould, historian on the subject, commented, 'built a wonderful house on sand, but Le Roy dug down to the rock'.

It was left to two Englishmen, bitter business rivals, to develop the practical marine chronometer. Up to now it had taken years to make a single marine timekeeper.

John Arnold and Thomas Earnshaw each made about thousand chronometers during their working lives a prices well below anything made previously. Arnold who had run away from his home in Bodmin, Cornwal had learned the craft in Germany and presented to Ger man-speaking King George III an amazing miniatur watch he had made. It was set in a finger ring yet had complicated mechanism repeating the hour and quarte on bells when required. It is doubtful if anyone today could make a duplicate. Arnold developed a deten escapement and set up a factory to make marin chronometers.

Earnshaw, who came from Ashton-under-Lyne, i Lancashire, had much the same temperament as Harrison of whom he said: 'a reward has been given more that six times the amount of that which I ask; and that to a person whose productions were an hundred time inferior to mine.' He said of Arnold, who was rathe pompous, 'if he was the first who applied gold springs.. it was because of the corrosive matter which... ouze from his hands rusted all the steel ones.'

Earnshaw was very poor when he started and had t get his timekeepers made by another craftsman, Wright who put his own name on them.

Berthoud, Arnold, and Earnshaw all developed deten

scapements. The detent escapement, the essence of the marine chronometer, has a distinctive tick as it lets the scape wheel jump at every other swing of the balance wheel, instead of at every swing like most escapements.

The Spanish government, after the defeat of their armada, was intensely interested in methods of improving navigation and tried to set up a government chronometer factory. They bought chronometers from John Arnold in England and Ferdinand Berthoud in France, and made an arrangement with Berthoud for him to train a Spanish apprentice, Cazetano Sanchez. Sanchez also studied with London chronometer makers.

He made remarkable progress, but alas, just after his return to Spain both he and his assistant, Cruzado, died in the plague of 1800. At the same time, a schoolfellow of Sanchez, called Antonio Molina, was sent to London to learn the art of jewelling, which was an English trade secret for many years. The Spanish government had discovered a watchmaker who was prepared to betray the secret to Molina for 100 guineas. Molina returned to Spain with the process in 1795. Two years later he went to Paris to buy some gems to convert and died suddenly while there. He was succeeded by Carlos La Rue, who died in 1800 in the same plague as Sanchez and Cruzado. Two more apprentices were sent to Berthoud for training which they completed after stormy apprenticeships. One of those died in another epidemic. The Tsar of Russia tried to tempt the other to Petrograd with his knowledge, but he stayed in Spain. The Spanish government had had enough bad luck, however. They closed the factory and bought chronometers from England and France.

Maskelyne's method of finding the longitude by lunar distances, although complicated, was in fairly common use until the 19th century. Despite their convenience, marine chronometers were slow in being accepted by more conservative seamen. Adventurers like Captain Cook were quick to realise their merits, but the Admiralty did not make a general issue until 1818. Before then navigators who wanted them had to buy their own.

Broadcasting of Greenwich Mean Time by radio revolutionised navigation in the 1920's. It was the ideal method of checking a chronometer at sea. Today, development of sophisticated navigational systems like Decca's are rendering the marine chronometer less essential. But in times of war, when radio blackout is essential, the marine chronometer still reigns supreme.

During the 19th and early 20th centuries there were large numbers of chronometer makers in London, who competed in the Chronometer Trials organised by the Admiralty for many years.

Very few makers are left – Thomas Mercer in England, Le Roy in Paris, and Ulysse Nardin in Switzerland. During the last war, Hamilton also made them in the USA.

Pierre Le Roy, of Paris, whose ideas founded the modern marine chronometer

Miniature finger ring watch by John Arnold which strikes the hours and quarters on a silver bell. It is said to be the one presented to George III in 1764
USHER COLLECTION, CITY OF LINCOLN

American shelf clocks by Chauncey Jerome HAGANS CLOCK MANOR MUSEUM, COLORADO

Clocks and watches in North America

The first clock and watch makers in North America came from Europe as settlers because they had been driven away by religious intolerance, or just because they sought adventure in the New World. They practiced their craft as they had been taught it as apprentices in England, Germany, Holland and elsewhere, and trained their own apprentices in the same way.

Although they were isolated from the changes taking place in Europe, the clocks they made could be taken for those of European make. One of the most popular productions was the English type of longcase clock. In fact few other styles were made until about 1800.

Probably the earliest American clock still extant is a longcase with a flat top by Abel Cottey, who emigrated with William Penn and started a business in Philadelphia in 1682. Styles of longcase clocks were little different from English productions except that an urn appeared in the spandrels, the metal corner ornament of the dial, instead of a cherub's head. After about 1760, almost all American longcase clocks had horned tops like those on English provincial cases, and from about 1790 these were

developed into a cut-out cresting not seen elsewhere and called 'whalestails'. Because metal was so short, however, the movements of many American clocks were made of wood and ran for thirty hours. Metal was saved for the better ones than ran for eight days.

Certain early clockmakers gained great eminence. Among them was David Rittenhouse, of Pennsylvania. Rittenhouse, with Benjamin Franklin who was a clockmaker of some merit, and John Winthrop, have been called the 'Fathers of the Revolution'. By the time he was seventeen years old, in 1749, Rittenhouse had established himself at Norriton as a maker of accurate clocks. Later he turned to astronomical clocks and orreries – models demonstrating the motion of the planets – and also moved to Philadelphia. He succeeded Benjamin Franklin as secretary of the American Philosophical Society, which was similar to the more ancient English Royal Society, and was himself succeeded by Thomas Jefferson. Rittenhouse was first Master of the American Mint, and built the first, and for many years the only, astronomical observatory in America.

It is little known that a French clockmaker played a crucial part in the American War of Independence. His name was Pierre Caron de Beaumarchais, a mechanic who became a brilliant watchmaker, inventor, politician, courtier much disliked by the hereditary ones, and librettist. He wrote 'The Barber of Seville' to the music of Mozart and 'The Marriage of Figaro' to that of Rossini.

Beaumarchais had so much influence with King Louis XVI that he managed, against the advice of the king's ministers, to obtain the support of France for the revolt of the American colonies under George Washington against English rule. A treaty to this end was negotiated by Benjamin Franklin in 1778. By his personal effort and money, Beaumarchais raised a fleet of forty vessels to help America, but because of the discreditable activities of Arthur Lee, the American Commissioner in France who took all the credit for himself, it was fifty years, and long after the death of Beaumarchais, that some compensation was paid by Congress against the personal fortune that Beaumarchais had spent.

One early maker was Thomas Claggett of Newport, Rhode Island, who was working from 1730 to 1749, and who had as an apprentice Thomas Harland of Norwich, Connecticut, who in turn was master to Daniel Burnap of East Windsor, Conn. All became famous, but it was Burnap's apprentice who left the biggest mark of all on American clockmaking. His name was Eli Terry and he was born in 1772 in East Windsor, in the 'Nutmeg State', which was yet to gain its reputation of being able to sell anything, even wooden nutmegs.

Eli Terry was apprenticed at the age of fourteen to Burnap. Probably he gained some learning from the many English and Hessian prisoners who were held in the area after the revolution. While Terry was learning how to cast brass and harden it by hammering, to file, drill and burnish brass and steel, George Washington became the first American President. The country was very short of copper and zinc for making brass, which came from England, and for that reason a number of makers had copied the methods of the Black Forest makers introduced by German immigrants and were making wooden clock movements.

Benjamin and Timothy Cheney produced wooden clocks in the next village, East Hartford, turning them out one at a time, like brass clocks of the time. The dials of these clocks were brass and the rest, including the wheels, of wood. One of the Cheneys taught woodworking to the Willard family, that afterwards became famous in American clockmaking. Eli Terry decided, or was sent, to work with the Cheneys after he was out of his apprenticeship.

Simon and Aaron Willard, of Massachusetts, made many fine longcase clocks and were responsible for introducing peculiarly American timekeepers known as a 'shelf clocks'. Small-sized longcase clocks – 'grandmother

American calendar clock, which also gives times of sunrise and sunset at the latitude of New England

clocks' – were made more often in America than in England, where 18th-century versions were very rare. They were probably favoured because they employed less material, and it might have been from this small standing clock that the 'Massachusetts shelf clock' was developed, like a chest on a chest of mahogany, usually under four feet tall. At this time the shelf clock followed no particular pattern and other makers, including David Wood, the Baileys, and makers in Concord, Mass. had their own variations.

At this time a favourite cheap clock was the hanging wall clock with a hood and a thirty-hour movement and exposed weights and pendulum, commonly known as 'the wag on the wall'. The Willards, however, specialised in high quality clocks. Some years later, in 1802, Simon Willard invented the banjo clock with a round dial, tapered trunk, and box shaped base, which although severe in style is probably the most attractive of all American clocks. Most banjo clocks show only the time, but some were made with alarms, the hammer striking the wooden case. Other makers copied the style and developed it into the lyre clock, following an earlier French style in which the sides of the trunk are curved and decorated by applied carving.

Another version of the banjo clock was the 'girandole' which has a circular instead of a rectangular base.

The Willards also made lighthouse clocks, novelty clocks shaped like lighthouses with dials in the 'lamphouses' but are said to have limited the number to thirty.

Returning to Terry, at the age of twenty-one he was making brass wheeled clocks bearing his own signature, but he left to settle in the thinly populated parish of

Beaumarchais, librettist and watchmaker, who also spent his fortune supporting the American War of Independence

Northbury thirty-five miles to the south-west where he had met a girl he was eventually to marry. The nearest clockmaker was Gideon Roberts making wooden wheeled clocks. At that time a clockmaker depended to some extent on the potential customers around him. They had to visit his workshop by horseback. There were few waggons. The clockmakers soon found, when they became short of money and could buy no more materials, that they had to go out after the customers, again following Black Forest practice. The usual way was by horse, carrying four movements, one in each saddle bag, one in the pommel and the other on the cantle of the saddle. Customers often did without clock cases, or bought them later.

Not every buyer had the cash to pay for a clock and offered to barter other goods for it. Terry recorded having taken two saddlebags of pork for a clock. He and other clockmakers began accepting IOU's, called 'clock notes'. Some clockmakers employed debt collectors to redeem them, which was difficult, and the notes had a low standing as negotiable currency.

About this time, another Yankee, Eli Whitney, after experiments with mass production methods, landed a government contract to produce a hundred thousand muskets in less than two years, which probably inspired Eli Terry.

The craftsman's method of production is for each man to make a complete clock or watch, fitting each part separately to its neighbours. A part from one clock will not necessarily fit another 'identical' clock made by another craftsman. This was developed into batch production by the English, German and French industries, when a group of craftsmen would concentrate on making certain parts as identical as possible. They would then concentrate on other parts and finally complete timepieces would be assembled from the parts, necessary adjustments being made during assembly.

In mass production, the process is taken a step further, with enough workmen continuously producing all the parts and assembling the complete clocks or watches without switching from one job to another. To make a complete clock therefore takes only as long as the longest single operation in making it, and clocks or any other manufactured articles can be turned out at fantastic rates. A modern alarm clock factory will produce complete going clocks at one every few seconds.

There was one big obstacle to producing clocks in quantity in Terry's day – finding enough customers to buy them, and pay for them. In the meantime, however, Terry, obsessed with his ideas, set up a water-powered workshop over a stream on a hill between Plymouth and

what is now Thomaston. His production, in batches of twenty-five, crept up to about two hundred a year.

In 1806, Napoleon blockaded the British Isles and cut off American shipping. Two brothers Porter in Waterbury, one a priest and the other a button maker, suddenly decided that in this protected market, they could build a big business as clock wholesalers selling to peddlers – provided that they could sell the clocks cheaply enough. They decided that Terry was the man to produce them and gave him an order for four thousand wooden grandfather clock movements. They said they would supply the oak, laurel and other materials, and gave Terry three years to complete the order.

It was Terry's chance. He sold his old mill and bought a bigger one from a carpenter named Calvin Hoadley. For a year he did nothing but plan and set up the new works. Then he put through a pilot batch of five hundred clocks and finished them well short of the next year. He also took on a young carpenter and joiner named Seth Thomas, whose job was to assemble parts into clocks. The Porters' order was finished on time.

During this period, he engaged Silas Hoadley, nephew of the man from whom he bought the mill, to work for him. For a time clocks were sold under the name of Terry, Thomas, and Hoadley. Terry sold out to Thomas and Hoadley in 1811 and went back to Plymouth Hill. These years saw many changes in partnerships. Terry's sons were now active in clockmaking, running three firms

Wooden 'grandfather clock' movement, one of many made by Joseph Ives of America after 1812
MR. J. E. COLEMAN, NASHVILLE, TENN.

under their names. In 1811, Terry acquired a house in Waterbury from the Porters, perhaps in part payment for the big clock order. He was experimenting with making complete clocks during the times of 1812 until 1814 when America was at war with Great Britain, in support of Napoleon.

Terry decided to cut down the size of the clock from grandfather clock size to shelf clock, but smaller than the Massachusetts shelf clock. His would be only about two feet, six inches high, about half as wide as the height, and as narrow as possible. The front door would be of painted glass. He decided to reduce the pendulum from the thirty-nine inches of the longcase clock to a half-seconds pendulum of about ten inches long, and devised a system of pulleys to make the weights work the full length of each side of the clock. His first short pendulum patent was dated 1816.

Seth Thomas sold out to Silas Hoadley and set up on his own in Plymouth and made a fortune. Eli Terry had another grist mill converted to a clock factory for his latest wooden wheeled shelf clock.

This thirty-hour clock was in a rectangular case abou twenty inches tall by fourteen inches wide and fou inches thick. The front was a glass panel on which th dial was painted so that the movement could be seen Soon dials were fitted with a hole in the middle and finall locally painted wooden dials were used. The early clock had the pendulum on the right. After 1823 the pendulum was moved to the centre.

The finest development of the shelf clock, which was purely American design, was the pillar and scroll case which may have originated from a design by Hema Clark, and was introduced by Terry in 1817. It has tw slender pillars, one each side, and narrow feet, with scrolled cresting at the bottom between the feet and swan neck pediments at the top with three finials. Th Terry shelf clock revolutionised the American industr and saw the end of the longcase clock. In five years, Terr was making six thousand a year at $15 each complet in their cases.

Terry also took on another young carpenter, name Chauncey Jerome, who, like Seth Thomas, and Simo

*BELOW: Tiffany Never-wind electric clock which had a torsion
pendulum that rotated, and was run from a battery. It was made
in some numbers up to the 1930's. The name has no connection wit*
the famous Tiffany's MR. J. E. COLEMAN, NASHVILLE, TENN.

his house in Plymouth to Eli Terry for a hundred mant(
clock movements and bought a small farm in Bristol fo
two hundred and fourteen complete clocks.

In the 1820's the brass mills that had supplied butto
makers began to manufacture enough brass to sell outside
Connecticut clockmakers started to turn from wood t
the traditional materials of their trade. Joseph Ives c
East Bristol patented a clock with tin-plated iron plate
and brass wheels, and later developed a clock almos
entirely made of brass.

Joseph Ives had previously been responsible for a ver
distinctive form of clock movement, in a shelf clock
He took a leaf spring of the kind used in the suspensio
of a horse-drawn wagon and employed it to power
clock instead of weights. The spring was fastened to th
bottom of the case and drove the clock through cords an

Hoadley, was also destined to be celebrated today as an
American clockmaking pioneer.

In the meantime, clockmakers all over Pennsylvania
and Ohio as well as Connecticut, copied the pillar and
scroll shelf clock and Terry had a lot of trouble trying
to maintain his patent.

In 1818 Terry sold a 'shop right' to Seth Thomas to
make his improved movement and Seth Thomas was
soon producing as many clocks as Terry himself. A few
years later so many small men were pirating Terry's
designs that he decided to frighten them as they were
too numerous to sue. He brought an action against his
friend Seth Thomas for making sixteen thousand clocks
without authority. After the publicity of this action
against a friend, the case was quietly dropped.

Clocks became so plentiful that they were now sometimes used as money. The wheel had turned a full circle
from the old 'clock note' days. Chauncey Jerome sold

evers. There were three main types, the thirty-hour usually in a wall clock, the one-day, and the eight-day usually in what are called 'steeple on steeple' shelf clocks. Birge and Fuller of Bristol made a number of wagon spring clocks under Ives' patents.

In 1833, Eli Terry retired with a large fortune and turned over the business to the eldest of his sons, Eli Terry Junior, who added lock making to the output of the factory in what was now called Terrysville, but in a few years the wooden clock business was all but finished and the lock making was not making a profit.

Chauncey Jerome introduced what he called a 'bronze and looking-glass clock' which was cheaper and ousted Terry's pillar and scroll clock. It had thick half pillars, bronze mounts, and a looking glass at the bottom door panel instead of a painted landscape. About 1830, another form of shelf clock, the ogee, also became popular. The great depression of 1837 all but finished the clock industry, still mostly dependent on wood. In the same year rolled brass was introduced.

Chauncey Jerome, coming upon a German brass clock movement, realised that by introducing a few modifications, he could make it cheaply in quantity from rolled brass produced by machine. Traditionally, clockmakers cast brass into sheets and hammered it flat. Jerome's brass clocks were produced by him and his brother in huge quantities from about 1838.

The Jerome brothers' success began to force Eli Terry Junior out of business. He had been ill for some time, and died while the pressure was on. Seth Thomas was infuriated with the changes forced on the industry by the Jeromes, but nevertheless, converted his business successfully to brass clockmaking.

In 1842, Chauncey Jerome's production was so high he began exporting brass clocks to England for $1.50 each (12s 6d at present rate of exchange) and was accused by the British of dumping at under cost, but in America he was selling clocks for 75 cents (6s 3d). Seth Thomas and other American makers also assaulted the British market and succeeded in damaging the English clockmaking industry.

The effort was too much for Jerome, however. He had a spectacular bankruptcy in association with the famous showman, T.P. Barnum.

Today there are big industries in Bristol, Thomaston, and Waterbury. Some clockmakers in America made watches as well as clocks, but not many of them.

Thomas Harland of Connecticut is reported to have been making two hundred watches a year not long after 1800, probably using English ébauches (raw movements).

Luther Goddard was another. He was originally a preacher, but had a mechanical gift and, perhaps after meeting Eli Terry, set up a watchmaking shop in Shrewsbury, Massachusetts, in 1809 when the import of foreign watches was banned. In 1815, the law was repealed, which forced Goddard out of business after he had made about five hundred watches. So he turned again to evangelism.

Henry and James F. Pitkin, of Hartford, Conn., started a business making watches by machine in 1838, but it was a failure almost from the start, and Jacob C. Custer of Norristown, Penn., produced watches between 1840 and 1845.

There were two pioneers who made more impact than any others. One was Edward Howard of Hingham, Massachusetts, who was born in 1813 and became an apprentice of one of the famous Willard clockmaking family, Aaron Willard Jnr. After his introduction to machine clockmaking he was fired to make watches by machinery, a very tricky operation. The other man was Aaron L. Dennison, from an old English family in Maine, who had learned watchmaking from the English and Swiss in New York and Boston, and had set up a small business in Boston. After visiting Eli Whitney's Springfield plant making rifles by machine, he became obsessed by the possibilities of making watches by similar methods.

By chance the two men met, were at once struck by the similarities of their ideas, and resolved on joining forces. In 1848, a Samuel Curtis made the number three and put up capital of $20,000. Dennison went to England and Switzerland to study the craft methods of these two big industries, and reported: 'It needs but slight acquaintance with our art to discover that the lower grade of foreign watches are hardly as mechanically correct in

Briggs rotary clock which was patented in 1855-1856 and made in quantity by E. N. Welch of Bristol, Conn. in the 1870's. The 'conical pendulum' turns in a circle. A glass dome fits over the top MR. WALLACE HEATON, LONDON

E. Howard locomotive clock that was used in an American railway engine cab from 1870-1880 MR. J. E. COLEMAN, NASHVILLE, TENN.

Time lock clocks for strong rooms were invented by James Sargent about 1873. This one was made by Seth Thomas about 1900 MR. J. E. COLEMAN, NASHVILLE, TENN.

their construction as a common wheelbarrow.'

On Dennison's return a small factory was started at Roxbury, called the American Horloge Company, which made about seven watches a day. Its name was changed on several occasions and eventually it became the Waltham Watch Co., when a new factory at Waltham was set up. It is America's oldest and the parent company of most of the others.

There were enormous difficulties, some that were anticipated, like the lack of dial makers and gilders, others that were financial and never solved, and some highly unlikely such as the occasion when New England workmen downed tools on religious grounds because the teeth of the small gears they were making were shaped like bishops' mitres.

Dennison has been called 'the Father of the American watch industry', but Edward Howard said of him, 'as a machinist and builder of watch machinery, Mr. Dennison was not a success.' Although he was eventually forced out of the company he helped to create, his influence had been greater than other watch pioneers'. At the age of sixty-two, when most men would have been prepared to rest, Dennison emigrated to England and set up a watch factory which did not survive and then the Dennison Watch Case Co. which lasted from 1874 to 1967. Dennison is buried in Birmingham near two pioneers of the Industrial Revolution, James Watt and Matthew Boulton.

Many ingenious men besides Dennison were trying to design watches that could be made mainly by machine, would perform satisfactorily, and would be cheap in price. Among them was an obscure watch repairer named

D.A.A. Buck, who had made a small model of a steam engine he had seen at the Centennial Exposition at Philadelphia in 1876, celebrating the hundredth anniversary of the declaration of American Independence. A man named Edward A. Locke, of Boston, who was trying to form a watchmaking company, saw the model and asked the watchmaker if he could design a watch for machine making.

Buck's second effort was eventually manufactured from 1880 by a company at Waterbury in Connecticut that was named the Waterbury Watch Co. The watch became probably the most famous of all early machine-made ones, because of the extreme originality of its design and the fact that it was so successful.

The entire watch movement rotated in the watch case, turning once in an hour and taking the watch hour hand with it. This is the tourbillon principle referred to in Chapter 4, to reduce errors caused by the position of the watch. The mainspring was coiled in the case around the movement, the escapement was a cheap form of duplex, the dial was of paper covered with a sheet of celluloid, there were only fifty-eight parts, and the price was $4 (33s 4d).

The 'long wind Waterbury' attracted many jokes. The mainspring of some was eleven feet long and when an owner of a watch became tired of winding he would pass it over to a friend to help. It is said that the more ingenious owners used to run alongside a fence holding the winding button against the fence!

The Waterbury Watch Co. made other watches but eventually failed partly because this watch was offered as a 'free gift' in huge quantities all over the world, particularly by clothiers, and became so associated with shoddy products that the public would not buy it.

Another American pioneer was Robert H. Ingersoll who was brought up on a farm and knew little about watches, but was inventive and a first class salesman. With his brother he set up in business selling novelties for a dollar each and started one of the first mail order businesses. Growing impatient with novelties he resolved to sell watches for a dollar each. The first was really a small noisy clock wound from the back, but next he made a contract with the Waltham company to make watches for him and originated the famous slogan: 'The watch that made the dollar famous.' Eventually he bought two factories. The company is now British.

Early American watches have small interest for the collector today compared with European ones of the same period. Yet American ideas of making watches by machinery were directly responsible for the rapid growth of world dominance of the Swiss watch industry subsequently. England and Switzerland were the great exporters of watches around 1850, and between them had captured most of the world's markets.

In 1876 M. Favre-Perret, a Swiss watchmaker, was invited to be a member of the International Jury on watches at the Centennial Exhibition at Philadelphia, mentioned earlier. He returned to Switzerland staggered by the American watch factories he had seen. Both the English and Swiss watch industries refused to believe that accurate watches could be made by machinery. Yet a Swiss technician reported on the performance of an American watch acquired by M. Favre-Perret, 'I am completely overwhelmed; the result is incredible. One would not find such a watch among fifty thousand of our manufacture.'

The Swiss awoke to the alarm. They sent watchmakers to study American methods, with the result that their industry survived and flourished. The huge communities of English watchmakers would not believe that machine-made timepieces with their poor visual quality would ever oust their fine watches, despite attempts at machine manufacture in England by Aaron Dennison and others.

The chief exponent of machine methods in England were Sir John Bennett, who owned a shop in Cheapside in London and set up the old figures of Gog and Magog over his shop as an advertisement, and Lord Grimthorpe, who designed 'Big Ben'. Bennett was howled down by watchmakers when he suggested introducing Swiss methods. But he was right and the manufacturing industry of sixty thousand craftsmen rapidly died despite the protection organisation, The British Horological Institute, that they formed in 1858 – but that still flourishes!

Incidentally, the Edison Institute Museum in the USA has a collection of clocks and watches from England housed in a building representing Sir John Bennett's old shop.

Court jester clock made in Italy in the 18th century, made of wood and gesso and painted. The man on the swing is the pendulum moving backwards and forwards. It is now in the USA
HAGANS CLOCK MANOR MUSEUM, COLORADO

Striving after accuracy

'Honest George Graham', the London clock and scientific instrument maker, invented a precision version of the anchor escapement in 1715. He called it the 'dead beat' because the seconds hand stopped dead at every second and did not recoil slightly like the seconds hand of an ordinary longcase clock.

He also invented a pendulum that carried a jar of mercury at the end instead of a metal bob. When the temperature changed, the mercury expanded upwards compensating for the rod expanding downwards, so the pendulum did not change in length. John Harrison, in Lincolnshire, also invented a pendulum compensated for temperature he called the 'gridiron'. Either of these pendulum used with the dead beat escapement gave longcase clocks an accuracy previously undreamed of.

Such clocks became known as 'regulators' because they were used to regulate other clocks and watches. Usually they have special dials with a long minute hand in the centre and shorter seconds and hour hands above and below it.

The regulator was set to time by an astronomical observation or by a visible signal from an observatory. Time was also distributed by individuals. A woman named Ruth Belville used to carry it to Clerkenwell clock and chronometer makers early in the 20th century by means of an Arnold pocket chronometer which she set by the Greenwich Observatory clocks.

Public clocks had been left well behind in the endeavours to increase accuracy, largely because the dials were large and exposed. But despite the fact that the clockmaking industry in Britain was beginning to feel the effects of competition in mid-19th century, there was still much inventive genius available. When a new clock was needed for the Palace of Westminster (the Houses of Parliament) then being built, Charles Barry, the architect, asked the clockmaker B. L. Vulliamy to prepare plans for a clock. Other clockmakers got to hear of this and objected, so the Astronomer Royal provided a specification which required that the clock should have four thirty feet wide dials (the final ones were smaller) and must be accurate to a second a day in striking the first blow of each hour. He also laid down that it must signal its time by 'the new telegraph' twice a day to Greenwich Observatory.

Vulliamy, a renowned clockmaker of his time, declared the conditions to be impossible, with hands weighing several hundredweights being exposed to high pressure from wind and snow. Another clockmaker, E. J. Dent

LEFT: *The precision of a modern mechanical wrist watch depends considerably on the hairspring. This hairspring is shown with a human hair and a match head. It is made of a compensated non-magnetic alloy called Isovar* SOCIETE DES FABRIQUES DE SPIRAUX REUNIES, SWITZERLAND

RIGHT: *Close-up of the glass record of the speaking clock used for the 123 (TIM) telephone service* H. M. POSTMASTER GENERAL

won the contract. The Astronomer Royal, G. B. Airy, asked a brilliant amateur horologist to supervise the building of the clock. This was a man named E. B. Denison, MA, QC, who later became Lord Grimthorpe, a man of extremely strong character, positive opinion, and arrogant and rude manner. But he was also a man who never accepted anything at face value without proof.

Trouble soon started. Grimthorpe ran foul of the government department which appointed the architect and civil engineers as referees. Dent, the clockmaker, could not stand the strain and retired. Shortly afterwards he died. There was an acrimonious battle before his stepson, Frederick Dent, could be appointed to carry on.

A continuous struggle was being waged between Grimthorpe and Barry as to whether the tower should be built for the clock or the clock for the tower. Barry wanted drawings of the clock and Dent told him they did not exist, so he went to the Astronomer Royal, who asked Grimthorpe to make some. Grimthorpe said he had no intention of doing so. The Astronomer Royal then resigned. Grimthorpe's comment was, 'As his knowledge of large clocks was purely theoretical, and not one of the suggestions he had made could be adopted, his resignation saved a great deal more of unprofitable correspondence.'

Grimthorpe had taken the precaution at the beginning to make sure that, as he put it, 'by the legal effect of the contract I had real power to direct the work...' As soon as this was discovered, 'every possible effort was made to get rid of it and me. No official who joined in those attempts cared three half-pence how the clock was made. Luckily I did care, and knew what would become of it if I gave up.'

He was right. He developed a special escapement for the clock known as a 'three-legged gravity escapement'. The thirteen foot pendulum is kept swinging by two arms, one at each side. The arms are raised alternately and released gently so that the weight of an arm bears on the pendulum rod to give it a gentle push in one direction. The other arm impulses it in the other direction. The result is that pressure on the hands caused by high winds, snow, or pigeons standing on them, cannot affect the pendulum and, as a result, the rate of the clock.

Grimthorpe also fancied himself as an expert on bells, and controlled the casting of the hour bell which was the largest ever cast in Britain, as it weighed sixteen tons.

It was brought from the Whitechapel Foundry to Westminster by river, being hauled over Westminster Bridge on a trolley drawn by sixteen horses, while the traffic was stopped and the crowds cheered. It was hung in the Palace yard and tested. After two weeks it cracked. Grimthorpe announced that the bell founder had filled holes caused by faulty casting with cement and the bell founder sued him for libel, but the case was not settled.

Another hour bell was cast and brought up the river the same way. It weighed less, thirteen and a half tons, and also developed a crack, although this has not much affected its tone. It was named 'Big Ben' after Sir Benjamin Hall, the Chief Commissioner for the government looking after the work.

Before the bells were installed there was trouble with the hands. Grimthorpe, 'rather unwillingly and with some misgiving', allowed the architect to design them. The first ones of cast iron, Grimthorpe said were of such frightful weight he would not allow them to be put on. The second ones were of gun metal and 'fell over a minute or two every time they passed the vertical'. Grimthorpe redesigned them and reduced the weight by over a half.

Fifteen years passed from the time plans were made

ABOVE: Complex carriage clock by J. F. Cole, 'the English Breguet'

RIGHT: English magic lantern clock made in 1810. It projects an image of the dial on the wall

Both clocks are in the BRITISH MUSEUM

THIS CLOCK WAS MADE IN THE YEAR OF OUR LORD 1854 BY FREDERICK DENT, OF THE STRAND AND THE ROYAL EXCHANGE, CLOCKMAKER TO THE QUEEN, FROM THE DESIGNS OF EDMUND BECKETT DENISON

FIXED HERE 1859

nd the clock was going in the tower with its quarter bells and hour bell, in 1859. It had been working in Frederick Dent's workshop for four years before it was installed because of the difficulties over the bells. A hardly-known fact is that Grimthorpe tried out his escapement in a small clock in Dent's workshop. This clock was later fitted in Cranbrook Parish Church in Kent, where it is still working.

Grimthorpe had a last dig at Sir Charles Barry, the architect. 'The cost of the bells, including £750 for recasting Big Ben, was under £6,000, while the cost of the iron frame provided by the architect was about £6,600, partly in consequence of its being made too weak at first, as I had told him that it would. And as the clock, with my hands, cost only £4,080, while his hands and dials alone cost £5,334, you will see that the actual clock and bells cost much less than the architect's appendages to them.'

One fact about this huge clock movement – it is sixteen feet long by five feet six inches wide – greatly upset clockmakers. The wheels were cast in iron and left rough, only the working surfaces being highly finished. Grimthorpe never missed a chance of pointing out that he prohibited all unnecessary polishing and reduced the cost of turret clocks by considerably more than half. 'I willingly accept what somebody said in derision of the Westminster clock – that it looks like a patent mangle, but still you know it goes better than any astronomical clock that was ever made.'

Grimthorpe was wrong about at least one thing. He declared: 'Anyone who sets to work to invent electrical clocks must start with this axiom, that every now and then the electricity will fail to lift anything, however small.' He was referring to the electric clocks shown at the Great Exhibition of 1851 by C. Shepherd, who had persuaded the Astronomer Royal, Sir George Airy, to have his system installed at Greenwich Observatory the previous year. There is still a Shepherd electric clock, with twenty-four-hour dial, installed in the wall by the main gate.

A Scotsman named Alexander Bain tried to have Shepherd's name removed from the dial as he said the clock infringed his patent, obtained with another clockmaker, Barwise, in 1840. Bain had invented a printing telegraph outfit which he showed to Sir Charles Wheatstone, the important Professor of Science at London University. He also explained his ideas on electric clocks.

Shortly afterwards Wheatstone had some information about his own electric clock ideas published in *The Literary Gazette*. Bain immediately wrote to the journal an illiterate letter of complaint, which the Editor published without editing. Wheatstone replied grandly, referring to Bain as a 'working mechanic formerly in my employ'. But Bain and Barwise successfully took legal action against him later and in 1844, *Mechanics Magazine* commented, 'We congratulate Mr. Bain... and we earnestly trust that neither pirates nor professors will again annoy him.'

The railways found Bain's idea of a master clock operating slave dials particularly suitable for stations, and the first system was set up at Crewe. Bain clocks were driven by an 'earth battery' – zinc and coke buried near each other in the earth, kept moist, and connected to the clock by wire. The Leclanché cell had not then been introduced.

It was being realised at this time that electricity was particularly useful for relaying time signals because there was negligible delay. Wheatstone had managed to measure

LEFT: The huge movement of 'Big Ben', the Palace of Westminster clock

RIGHT: Lord Grimthorpe, designer of 'Big Ben'

A part of the very complex and highly accurate astronomical clock made by Jens Olsen and completed in the year 1944-1945. It is now in the Copenhagen Hall, Denmark

the speed of electricity and found it to be the same as the speed of light.

The old method of listening to a bell sound the hour was not accurate enough for ship's captains, for example, wishing to check their chronometers, because sound travels so slowly through the air. For this reason a device named a 'time ball' was invented by the Astronomer Royal, John Pond, and installed at Greenwich Observatory in 1833. The ball had a wooden framework about five feet in diameter, covered with leather. It was wound up a mast and released by a hand-operated trigger so that it dropped down the mast at precisely one o'clock every day. Seamen in the Thames, and chronometer makers as far away as Clerkenwell, could observe it to set their chronometers to time.

Airy, who followed Pond, linked the time ball with the new electric telegraph system being run by private companies and the railways. Later he installed Shepherd's electric clock, which caused the time ball to drop automatically. Time was distributed from Greenwich via the Electric Telegraph Co., to London and over the railway systems telegraph service to other places by an apparatus known as a 'chronographer'. At the telegraph offices, all work stopped at two minutes before certain hours so that the 'time current' could be received.

Deal installed a time ball and Shepherd clock in 1855,

and was followed by Devonport, Portsmouth, and Portland.

The first regular radio time signals were transmitted early in 1914 before the First World War from a German station at Nordeich and also from the French station on the Eiffel Tower in Paris. Clockmakers in England built crystal sets to receive them. When the war broke out however, the sets were confiscated. Regular broadcasting began in the United Kingdom on 15th November, 1922 and it became the custom of the announcer of the general news bulletin to play the Westminster chimes of 'Big Ben' on the studio piano as the time signal, taking his time from the studio clock. Later, a set of tubular bells was installed for this purpose.

On 21st April, 1923, Frank Hope-Jones, electric clock pioneer, gave a five minutes talk 'Alter Your Clock' about the Daylight Saving Act, which had become law the previous year. He announced the time he finished by vocalising the six seconds to ten o'clock by his watch. It was a novel idea and about a year later Hope-Jones and the Astronomer Royal, Sir Harold Spencer-Jones, devised a method of broadcasting the pips automatically through a telephone wire from Greenwich Observatory to the broadcasting studio at Savoy Hill.

The chimes of 'Big Ben' were broadcast as part of New Year celebrations on 31st December, 1923, and aroused such interest that the last quarter and nine strokes at nine o'clock became a regular time signal until 8th September, 1960, when they were discontinued. Records taken at Greenwich show that 'Big Ben' is incredibly accurate for such a large turret clock. Its average error is less than one fifth of a second a day.

France was first to put domestic electric clocks on the market in any quantity from early in the 20th century. One was a pendulum clock in a glass case using Bain's principle, and called a Bulle clock. The other was the Eureka, which has a very large balance wheel. One of the most successful early electric clocks was invented by a Swiss clockmaker named Matthaus Hipp, who used a little toggle to switch on the current only when the swing of the pendulum began to fall off. This brilliant idea of supplying electricity 'on demand' doubled the life of the Leclanché cells.

As early as 1894, Frank Hope-Jones had suggested that the alternating current of electricity supplies could be employed for timekeeping. At the time, however, the law required an accuracy equal to only about half an hour a day in the mains frequency. The man who made a practical mains clock was an American, Henry Ellis Warren. In 1918 he invented an electric motor that would keep in step with the mains frequency and drive clock hands. It was made under the name of Telechron. In the UK, the Smith's synchronous electric clock run off the mains, and introduced after the electricity grid system had been spread through the country, kept the clockmaking industry alive between the two world wars.

Frank Hope-Jones's biggest contribution was to make the electric clock extremely accurate. He perceived, like Grimthorpe, that the pendulum had to be freed from all extraneous work if it were to be really precise. He rejected early schemes, like Bain's, of driving the pendulum from the battery and the clock from the pendulum. Instead, he impulsed the pendulum by a gravity arm, like 'Big Ben's' pendulum. The electric current merely raises the arm into position and the weight of the arm gives the pendulum an impulse. Thus the state of the battery and variations in current do not affect timekeeping. His system is much more simple than the mechanical gravity escapement devised by Grimthorpe. The hands of the clock are also driven by pulses of electricity, the time of the pulses being decided by the pendulum, which rotates a tiny count wheel, the only work it does.

The idea of a pendulum that did no work was occupying the mind of another man, an engineer named W. H.

TOP RIGHT: Movement of a Eureka electric clock with its big balance wheel. The battery is in the base

RIGHT: The Bulle battery clock which has a Leclanché cell in the pillar and an electro-magnetic pendulum

ABOVE: *Floral clock by Smiths Industries in Roundwood Park, Willesden, London, which contains thirty-five thousand dwarf plants, two thousand of which are in the hands. It is eighteen feet in diameter*

RIGHT: *Two atomic clocks at the National Physical Laboratory, Teddington, England. The vertical tube in the foreground is the main part of the present standard clock. The trolley is an experimental clock* NATIONAL PHYSICAL LABORATORY

Shortt, who was in touch with Hope-Jones. The astronomical observatories were using accurate Rieffer pendulum clocks, but needed more and more accurate timekeeping and Shortt thought that the solution lay in freeing the pendulum. Eventually the inspiration came and he spent his Christmas holiday in 1922 installing his free pendulum clock in Edinburgh Observatory. It was extremely successful and many were made for other observatories. Some have kept time to less than a tenth of a second a year. One, belonging to a British Admiral, was responsible for his discovering that the earth wobbles on its axis, which affects its timekeeping.

The principle of the Shortt free pendulum clock is to use two pendulums. One, the free pendulum, is enclosed in a vacuum cylinder which is fixed as immovably as possible on a large concrete base not affected by vibration.

Combined with the free pendulum is a slave pendulum. There is a highly ingenious electrical linkage between the pendulums which keeps the free pendulum swinging

and enables it to accept an impulse only when it is ready for it. The circuit also keeps the slave pendulum in step with the free pendulum. The slave pendulum does all the work of counting the swings of the free pendulum, operating electrical circuits, and controlling the dials showing time. The free pendulum, relieved of all work, swings with the absolute minimum of interference.

The next step in extreme precision timekeeping was the replacement of the pendulum by a quartz crystal. The crystal is simply a wafer or ring of the mineral called rock crystal, cut to a predetermined size and shape. It is connected in an electronic circuit in such a way that it physically vibrates. Its vibrations controls the frequency of the electrical oscillations in the circuit, which can be used to operate clock hands. The quartz crystal – synthetic crystals which are purer than natural ones, are sometimes used now – acts in the same way as a balance or pendulum.

Quartz crystal clocks, invented in 1929 by W. A.

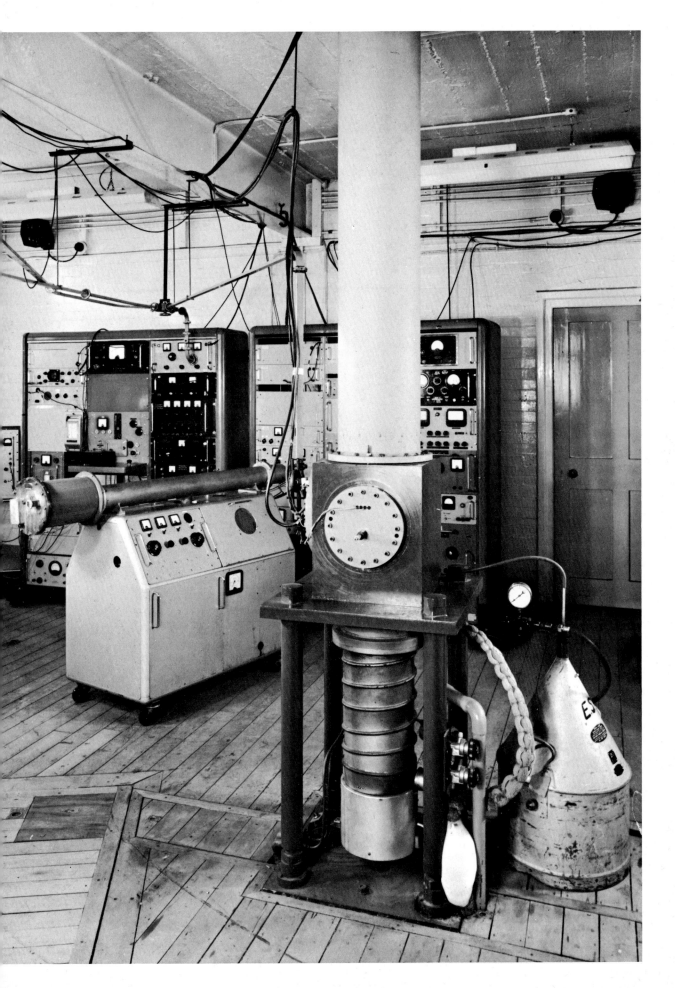

Marrison, a Canadian working for Bell Laboratories in the USA, will keep time to the equivalent of one second in thirty years, and have replaced free pendulum clocks in observatories. Because some crystals tend to drift in rate, quartz crystal clocks are normally employed in groups to detect this effect.

In 1955 Louis Essen and J. V. L. Parry, of the National Physical Laboratory in England, introduced an atomic clock in which the 'pendulum' was the vibrating atoms of the metallic element, caesium. The frequency of caesium is 9,192,631,770 cycles a second – a long, long way from the frequency of George Graham's 18th century regulators, half a cycle a second. Modern atomic clocks keep time to an equivalent of one second in three thousand years. Quartz and atomic clocks have shown that the Earth is slowing down. Its rate of spinning on its axis is reducing by about two thousandths of a second a year.

Atomic clocks are used to monitor other types of clocks and time signals. Portable ones have been made that can be carried in aircraft to different parts of the world for comparing quartz clocks at satellite tracking stations and in navigational transmitting stations. Generally, the larger the atomic clock, the more accurate it is.

Several countries are currently concentrating their technical efforts on reducing the size of quartz crystal clocks, particularly the Swiss, Japanese, and Germans. The quartz clock or watch is going through the same phase as the precision clock and watch in John Harrison's time in the 18th century, because intensive efforts are being made to reduce its temperature errors.

Some of the Swiss versions of domestic quartz clocks take electronic circuits to their logical conclusion and omit all mechanical parts, including moving hands. Time is shown by a series of flashing lights round a conventional dial or by illuminated figures.

Over the last six thousand or so years, man has used many natural phenomena and many ingenious and unusual devices to measure the passage of time, but he still does not know what time is. Even the absolute nature of time was successfully challenged by Albert Einstein.

In 1905, he predicted that a moving clock would run slow just because it was moving. After completing a trip and returning to its starting point, it would have lost time compared with a clock that had remained at the starting point. The difference is extremely small unless relative speeds are extremely high.

An ingenious double 'clock' made by the UK Atomic Energy Research Establishment at Harwell proved the theory to be true in 1960. The Harwell experiment employed a flywheel with a piece of radio-active substance near the axis and a similar piece near the rim. The 'ticks' of these two 'nuclear clocks' could be compared by using the Mossbauer effect, discovered by a German scientist, which makes it possible to measure the difference between an atom vibrating at 1,000,000,000,000

times a second and another vibrating at 1,000,000,000,001 times a second an incredible feat.

It was found that the clock at the rim, travelling at about five hundred miles an hour, ran slower than that at the centre. The loss was only three seconds in a million years – not enough to excite astronauts about perennial youth, but serious enough to physicists.

RIGHT: Quartz crystal electronic clock without moving parts by Soltronic of Switzerland. The time is shown by illuminated bars

BOTTOM LEFT: Clocks with transistorised movements driven by a battery made by Technical Executives and Smiths of England

BELOW: Clock driven by daylight or artificial light, by Kienzle of Germany. The solar cell on top draws enough energy from the light to keep the clock battery charged

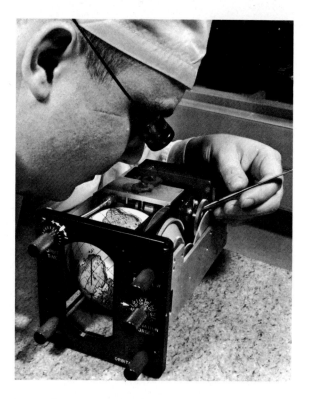

Users and uses

First users of timekeepers were perhaps early authorities – religious sects, armies, governments, but they may have been astronomers. When clocks were later introduced for public use they tended to become more decorative, with coloured astronomical dials and jacks. As they invaded the private house, they became also articles of furniture and at times more effort was lavished on their embellishment than on their functioning.

Astronomers and their assistants were most serious users and were also responsible for the most significant inventions – the pendulum clock and the watch balance spring – but gradually the field of endeavour moved to the specialist craftsmen and then to the horological engineer.

Today micro-electronics specialists are the men from whom the next generation of timekeepers can be expected. These men are also among the most serious users of accurate time, because as space technologists also, they demand extreme precision. A few millionths of a second make many miles difference in aiming deep space probes.

Precision much greater than that available to astronomers two generations ago is available to the ordinary householder today. He can have a chronometer movement driven by a transistorised motor, as in the Secticon clock; an electro-mechanical oscillator running off a battery; or a quartz crystal oscillator driving orthodox clock hands.

The off-shoot of the clock – the watch – more or less began life as a bauble rather than a serious timekeeper, but, as a pocket watch in the 18th century, started to challenge the clock in accuracy.

As a wrist watch in the 20th century, its development has been so rapid that watches compete with clocks in many present day circumstances, despite the fact that they are smaller, always being moved, and are often subject to greater extremes of temperature.

ABOVE: Astronaut's Earth path indicator by Minneapolis-Honeywell, a type of clock showing the movement of the Earth underneath him as if he were looking at it

TOP RIGHT: Electronic equipment by Greiner of Switzerland for positional timing and other checks on watches in manufacture. Each side is a watch rate recorder, as also used by repairers. The central instruments measure the swing of the balance wheel. In the centre is a watch on the microphone

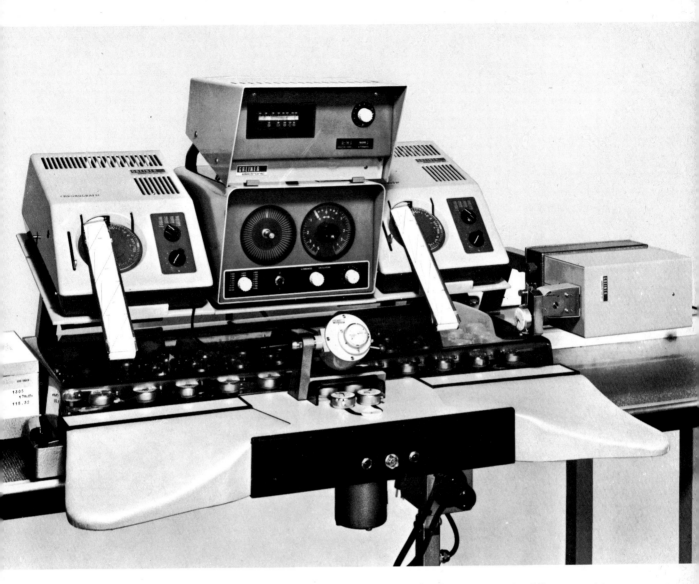

The latest watch prototype, announced in December 1967 by the Swiss Horological Electronic Centre is a miniaturised quartz crystal oscillator. It is said to keep time to within thirty seconds a year, ten times more accurate than current record holders in the same category. One reason is that it is not affected by 'positional errors'.

The difficulties of reducing a mechanism in size are obvious. Less obvious is the effect of the timekeeper being frequently moved. John Harrison spent his life overcoming this problem, among others, in sea clocks. A domestic clock stays in one place and the bigger and heavier it is, the less likely it is to be disturbed by anyone winding it or cleaning around it. Therefore it settles down to a relatively steady performance.

A pocket watch, too, is reasonably large and is usually kept upright in a fairly tight pocket where it stays at a comparatively even temperature. But a wrist watch is nearly always on the move, taking up different positions for short times when its owner is working, gesticulating, playing golf, digging, walking, and so on. Advantage of this fact is taken in the self-winding wrist watch.

No mechanical oscillator has ever been designed that will run at exactly the same rate in different positions. A watch will run at one rate when on its back and another on its side. The positions in which watch adjusters check the rate of a good wrist watch are: dial up, dial down, pendant up (i.e. winding button up with the dial facing the adjuster), pendant down, and pendant left. These positions are referred to as DU, DD, PU, PD, and PL.

The pendant right position is omitted from wrist watch testing because a wrist watch is never or hardly ever PR when the wrist watch is worn in the orthodox way, on the outside of the left wrist. Pocket watches and eight-day watches are tested in all positions except PD because they are very rarely used with the winder pointing downwards.

There are various official tests for timekeepers, the most rigorous ones generally being controlled by observatories. The Swiss have also set up special testing bureaux. All these authorities issue certificates. The most famous certificate of some years before the Second World War was the 'Kew A', issued by the National Physical Laboratory in the UK. Now the best known is that issued by the Swiss Bureaux which entitle a wrist watch to be

called a 'chronometer' although it does not have a chro
nometer (detent) escapement.

To gain a certificate, a watch must be tested for tw
days in each of the five positions. It must maintain a mea
daily rate between one and fifteen seconds fast, and hav
an average daily variation of not more than seven second
in the various positions. Refrigator and oven tests follow
after each of which the watch is re-checked at room tem
perature. It has to vary by not more than a certai
amount in each case and return to its original rate withi
certain limits.

In wear, the performance of a watch is an average c
different rates when the watch changes position. The fac
that a watch may go for months without having to rese
the hands to time of day is a tribute to the remarkabl
skills of the designers and adjusters.

When a fine watch has been adjusted, the worst error
will be found in the pendant right position, because it
PR positional error does not count in tests. Having th
latitude is of great assistance to the adjuster. Makin
adjustments to improve timekeeping in one positio
affects the timekeeping in others so he 'squeezes' th
worst errors into the PR position.

The result is that a watch worn on the inside of th
left wrist or on the outside of the right wrist gives it
worst performance. If it is necessary to wear the watc
on the inside of a wrist, it should be on the right on

Positional errors are caused by several factors. One i
that friction in the bearings of the balance wheel varies
normally being less when the watch is dial up or down i
a high quality watch. Another is that the centre of grav
ity of the balance and spring moves in a heart-shape
path as the balance wheel swings from side to side.
good watch that runs a few seconds fast may sometime
be brought to time by leaving it on its side at night.

Many of the latest higher quality watches have 'fas
train' movements and tick twice as fast as an orthodo
watch – ten instead of five times a second. This reduce
their positional errors and almost invariably they ar
excellent timekeepers. The poorer the quality of a wris
watch, the worse the positional errors.

Even a tuning fork watch has positional errors, bu
they are small and predictable, which is one of the reason
for the fine timekeeping performance. The only difference
in rate are in two positions when the tines of the fork ar
pointing up (losing) and when they are pointing down

*TOP LEFT: Stop watch by Breitling for use in
television and radio production. The outer scale shows feet of
35 mm or 16 mm film consumed*

*LEFT: Wrist watch timer for referees by Heuer-Leonidas.
The thin hand shows fifths of a second. The thick one shows
minutes on the outer scale which can be rotated to set the hand
against the number of minutes to go*

wards (gaining).

All mechanical watches and clocks are affected by changes in the weather, i.e. changes in barometric pressure, which affect the rate of the swinging of the pendulum, balance, tuning fork, or other oscillator. Some ingenious systems have been applied to correct barometric error in high precision pendulum clocks.

The most simple solution is the best, to eliminate the cause of the trouble, the air, and to seal the pendulum in a vacuum chamber. The same principle is employed in some watches. The vacuum watch has a sealed case from which the air is exhausted.

Vacuum watches do not suffer from another modern watch complaint, condensation on the inside of the glass. It has become a problem with watches, as with modern vehicles, since both have been more effectively sealed and there are fewer 'draughts' inside.

Condensations shows as a mist or milky film on the inside of the watch 'glass'. It can occur in watches that are completely watertight as well as those that are not. In a waterproof watch, the condensation comes from the minute amount of air sealed in the watch and is too small to cause any damage. A watch that is not watertight, however, is constantly 'breathing' air in and out as the temperature changes. The changing air can cause more and more moisture to be deposited inside as condensation. The result is rust and damage.

A cause of faulty timekeeping that has plagued clock and watchmakers for centuries is lubricating oil. Almost all mechanical timepieces are started and stopped at every tick. Starting one or more times every second takes up energy. Too much friction in the bearings can cause a timepiece to stop between ticks. To reduce friction and wear that might increase friction, steel pivots usually run in brass or synthetic ruby bearings and the bearings are oiled. It is the oil that causes the trouble because it causes the friction to vary.

As a timepiece is expected to work over many years without the bearings being cleaned or the oil changed, the oil inevitably becomes oxidised so that it grows gummy or soapy. A soapy oil does not matter as much as the fact is that it will probably have picked up some dust from the air unless the movement is a hundred per cent sealed. Dust usually includes tiny particles or quartz – like flint – which is harder than steel. It forms a grinding paste with the dried up oil and scores the bearings of the watch or clock.

A difficulty of the designer and workshop is to keep the oil in the correct places for long periods of time. On most parts of the movement, such as the teeth of the trains of gears, oil does more harm than good. The amateur almost invariably oils the wheel teeth of clocks and watches, which is quite wrong. The professional places a smear only on the teeth of the escape wheel. Oil, in measured amounts, is for the bearings.

A small amount of oil in the wrong place – a certain part of a gravity escapement – can stop even a huge turret clock movement.

The first lubricants used on clocks were probably animal fats (particularly tallow) and olive oil. Neatsfoot oil was favoured in England and porpoise oil in America. Neatsfoot is called 'cowheel oil' in some parts of the world. Porpoise oil actually comes from the head of this fish. There is a story of a great storm at sea which landed hundreds of porpoises on the beach at New Brunswick earlier in the century and provided a firm making the oil with stocks for many years. It is still made and used today.

The invention of the steam engine and then the internal combustion engine led to rapid development of an oil industry, producing lubricants from natural crude oil. It had little impact on clocks and watches because mineral oils tend to spread, whereas fatty animal oils will remain in drops where they are placed. Most watch and clock oils are blended from combinations of mineral and animal oils.

A fatty oil can oxidise, become sticky, then gum up and become so hard and resinous it is difficult even to remove. To avoid ageing, various synthetic oils for clocks and watches have been developed over recent years after

Watch for executives with business in two time zones and also, in this case, for Muslims a long way from Mecca so that they can follow religious rites by the time there

Skin divers' watch by Nivada which has a gauge around the dial to indicate depth down to six hundred and sixty feet. It also has a calendar!

mechanisms. Manufacturers today have gone some way along the path, however, by developing metals that are self-lubricating. In the electronic timepiece the lubrication troubles are being solved in a different sense, by eliminating most, or all, moving parts that need lubrication.

The watch and clockmaker is also a serious user of time. He must have a standard timekeeper against which he can rate the clocks and watches he makes or repairs. In the 18th and 19th centuries, he used a particularly accurate clock which he checked from time to time against a sundial, correcting with the equation of time, after the difference of clock and sun times was discovered. For more accurate work, he would check his clock against the transit of a clock star on successive nights and correct for the difference between sidereal and mean solar times.

Later, time services were provided by the Greenwich Observatory and private companies and then the British Broadcasting Company offered universal time signals. However, the clock and watchmaker still maintained his own master timekeeper, which was normally a regulator clock or a marine chronometer, rated against time signals.

To regulate any timepiece passing through his hands he would set it to time against his own master clock and then check and regulate it as necessary every twenty-four hours until it reached the standard of timekeeping required. Such an adjustment takes a minimum of three days and usually much longer if some degree of precision is required. John Harrison took three years to regulate his sea clock H3!

Since the Second World War, a new form of time standard for checking clocks and watches has come into rapid use. It has speeded up the process from days to minutes and made a profound impact on the manufacture of watches and clocks. It is known as the 'watch rate recorder', or less accurately the 'watch timer'.

Essentially, the rate recorder is a quartz crystal clock of high accurayc. Instead of showing time on a dial, the quartz oscillator feeds out a strip of paper from a reel at a very precise rate. A watch under test is fitted to a special microphone which amplifies the ticks and causes them to be printed as small dots or dashes on the moving paper. Another form of microphone can be clipped to a clock with the same results.

If the watch is accurate, the dots are printed in a straight line down the centre of the paper strip as it emerges. If it is fast or slow, the line of dots slopes to the left or the right. The angle of the slope can be read off a scale in seconds or minutes of losing or gaining a day.

The watch and microphone can be turned on the microphone stand to record the rate of the watch in different positions. Positional errors can therefore be found after tests lasting minutes instead of weeks, which is of great help to the watch adjuster. The adjuster still requires much understanding to estimate how the rate will average in wear, especially as this differs to some

research in several countries. They have many uses, but have not yet ousted the classical blended oils.

One of the most important oiling discoveries was made by the French horologist Paul Ditisheim, in the 1920's. He found that stearic acid could be used as a coating on metals and would prevent oil from spreading. He called it the 'epilame' process. Most factories now epilame their watches and advanced watch repairers use the process after cleaning by ultrasonic equipment.

The difficulty with epilame films is that they are very thin and present problems when applied to watch jewel bearings. In 1956, a Swiss chemist, Dr. Oswoiecki, invented a process which modified the surface of the ruby jewel and gave better and more lasting results than epilaming with stearic acid. It was first applied to watch shock absorbers.

A complete solution to timekeeping problems caused by oil would be to eliminate it, as John Harrison did with the first three of his sea clocks in the 18th century, but this has not proved practicable, especially with smaller extent from person to person.

The latest machines in Swiss watch factories not only provide a time standard, but automatically measure the rate of balance and hairspring assemblies, adjust the length of the hairspring until the rate is accurate, cut it off and pin it up ready for fitting to the watch – a task that previously called for very high human skills. More orthodox watch rate recorders are used to check the assembled watches to make sure that the automated machine has carried out its task accurately .

A watch rate recorder gives the 'instantaneous rate' of a timepiece, but cannot indicate that the timepiece will maintain that rate over a longer period. When checking chronometers and deck and wrist watches used in navigation where long term accuracy is essential, a modification of the traditional method is employed, called the audiovisual technique.

In the Chronometer Branch of the Hydrographer of the Navy at Hurstmonceaux Castle, Sussex, for example, there is a large room containing marine chronometers on test. All are set to time against a slave dial operated from the Royal Greenwich Observatory, that sounds short pips at the seconds and longer ones at half and full minutes. The chronometers are checked every twenty-four hours and their rates recorded by two specialists who compare the times shown with the audible signal. They can check to a tenth of a second a day in this way.

Both the short and the long methods are ingeniously built into Smiths factory in Scotland making low-priced alarm clocks. After the clocks have been regulated with the help of rate recorders, they are set to six o'clock – not time of day – and placed on a moving belt which travels round the factory in exactly twenty-four hours so that, as each clock arrives back at its starting point twenty-four hours later, it should show six o'clock again, or just after six, according to the tolerance permitted.

Many modern appliances have timepieces or time standards built into them. The automatic oven switch is based on a synchronous electric clock. The automatic toaster has in effect, a 'thermal clock'. The camera delayed timer is a simple clock mechanism, as is the delayed action of some automatic towel dispensers. Parking meters are clocks. Street lighting is controlled by time switches that compensate for differing lengths of darkness at different times of the year.

Traffic lights have built-in time devices – electronic usually, depending on the charging and discharging of capacitors. A similar method is the basis of some electronic photographic timers, although most are mechanical. The Midas 'black box' recorder fitted to big jet aircraft is based on a mechanical clock. This records information on a magnetic tape about the airframe and engine during flying. The object is for the tape to be played through after landing and print out information about maintenance required. The hours of flying information can be exam-

Watch by Favre-Leuba showing height above sea level or barometric pressure for climbers and fliers. It is set to one or the other before setting out and continues to give a correct reading

ined in a few minutes. Another is to provide crash information.

The digital computer relies upon its own 'clock' or time base for all the calculations it performs. It converts all information into binary numbers which employ only two symbols, 1 and 0. These are represented by an electronic pulse or blip (1), and the absence of a pulse or blip (0). Sequences of blips representing numbers or items of information pass through the circuits of the computer with the speed of light or are held in the computer's memory as magnetic spots or absence of spots.

The intervals of time during which a blip is sent or not are the 'ticks' of an electronic clock within the computer. It 'ticks' at a rate of about a million times a second, so a computer word such as 10010110101 (which is 1205 in ordinary decimal numbers) takes about eleven millionths of a second to handle in an electronic computer.

Even the ordinary wrist chronograph can be provided with a scale enabling it to be used as a simple computer. A stop watch is a pocket watch which can be stopped

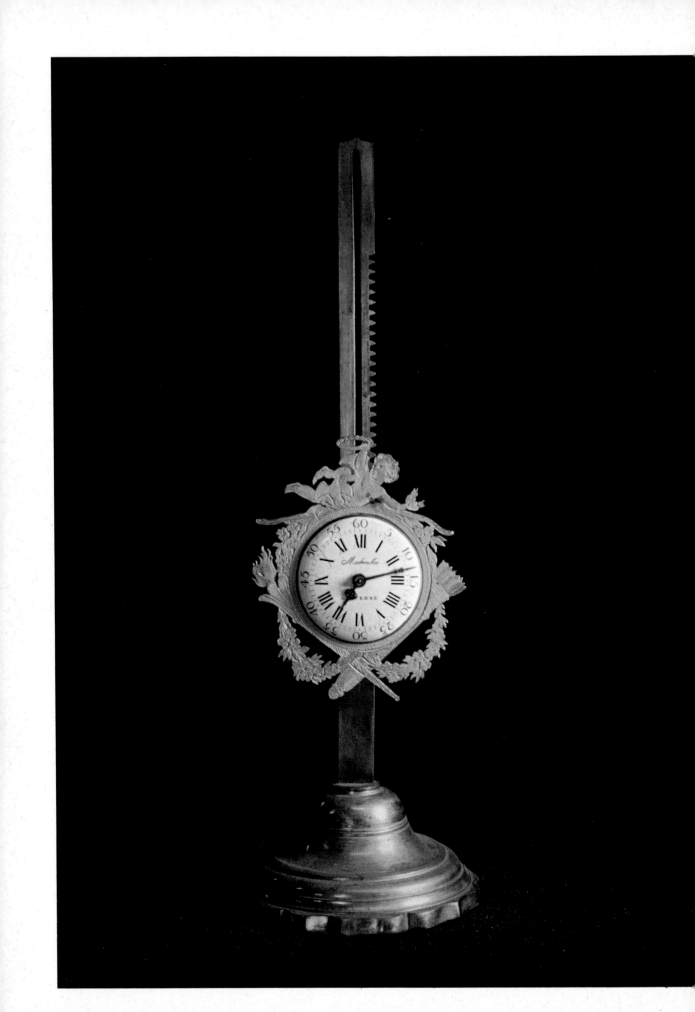

*LEFT: A trick rack clock of c. 1780. The clock is actually
spring-driven and climbs up the rack instead of descending*

*ABOVE: Four miniature 'jockele' clocks made in the Black Forest
of Germany and in Austria, in the 18th century*

All these clocks are in the BRITISH MUSEUM

Dashboard clock and timer for car rallying, by Heuer. The timer, on the right, shows hours, minutes and seconds to 1/5th, and will add periods of time. The marker is on the bezel which, can be turned

and started and shows only intervals of time; a chronograph is an ordinary time-of-day watch that is combined with a stop watch. Most chronographs today are also wrist watches.

When a logarithmic scale is added to the dial of a chronograph, the chronograph hand will perform a simple mathematical operation. A typical version is the tachymeter, which shows the average velocity of a moving object. If a motor vehicle, for example, is timed over a mile, the chronograph hand will indicate the speed in miles an hour. Timed over a kilometre it will indicate the speed in kilometres per hour, and similarly, of course, over other distances. Some are scaled for quarter miles or kilometres.

The same system is involved with the telemetre dial. If the watch hand is started when the flash of a gun is seen, and stopped when the sound is heard, the reading

will give the distance away of the gun. The production timer giving hourly production rates after timing the production of a single item, the pulsemeter for measuring the rate of pulse beats, and the sculling timer for strokes per minute, all invoke the same principle.

Divers' watches and many sports watches have bezels (rims) that can be rotated. The bezel is marked with twelve hours, or with sixty minutes or seconds, or both. It can be turned until one of the hands points to zero. The hand will then show the elapsed time from that moment in hours, minutes, or seconds according to which hand is involved. On some bezels, the scales go contraclockwise. The bezel is turned so that a hand points to the required interval – say of the time an air bottle will last under water; the hand will then show the reducing amount of time left, down to zero.

As well as the now common calendar and alarm watches

DISCIPLINE 07 SERIE 1
NAPOLI 28 SEPTEMBRE 1963
OMEGA Ω OMEGA

Print from an Omega camera timer showing the end of a sprint and the chronograph times along the bottom edge. The runners never appear like this as they are actually photographed one after the other (through a slit on moving film) in the same place

(some designed as parking meter timers), there are decimal dial watches for engineers and twenty-four-hour dials for travellers and pilots (some combined with a world time bezel giving the time in principal cities in other countries).

Many watches incorporate separate devices related to the use of the watch. For engineers and navigators, there is one with a combined slide rule; for skin divers one with a depth meter, and for walkers, mountaineers and pilots one with an altimeter and another with a compass.

Stop watches and chronographs are made for almost every use – yacht racing, boxing, shooting, rugby, rowing, fencing, horse racing, ice hockey, mining, navigating, oil refining, projectile timing, psychology testing, rallying, radio and TV production, and so on.

Most modern watches are protected to a reasonable extent against the effects of magnetism because the hair-

spring and balance are 'anti-magnetic', but old watches with steel hairsprings or balances made partly of steel can be badly affected. There are high strength magnetic fields around television circuits and many modern kitchen gadgets employ magnets.

Most watch repair shops are equipped with demagnetisers which operate by applying a rapidly alternating magnetic field to the watch or watch parts. The field reduces quickly in strength, leaving only the very slightest residual magnetism in the watch. Engineers working in high magnetic fields can obtain a wrist watch which has a special protective shield around the movement.

Despite the fact that watches are unaffected by ordinary magnetic fields, there is still a well-entrenched belief that some people cannot wear watches without upsetting the timekeeping. The 'victim' usually declares that his watch stops 'because of the magnetism in his body'.

There is no foundation whatever for this belief and all attempts to prove it have failed.

The idea of 'human magnetism' or 'animal fluid' came from the experiments of Mesmer, which are today called hypnosis. The body does have slight electrical potential differences over the autonomic nervous system, which are employed in the medical practice of acupuncture, but they are so tiny that the magnetic fields they set up are only a few thousandths of that caused by the Earth's magnetic field.

The Earth's magnetic field, which causes the compass to swing, has an effect even on a non-magnetic watch to the extent of tenths of seconds a day.

The non-magnetic balance spring was invented by the Swiss metrologist, Dr. C.E. Guillaume, who had earlier, in 1898, developed a metal he called Invar (from *invariable*) for pendulum rods that hardly varied in length with changes of temperature. Invar greatly increased the accuracy of pendulum clocks and eliminated the complicated temperature compensation system.

His balance spring had a constant elasticity in different temperatures and he called it Elinvar, from *élasticité invariable*. It also could be used without complicated temperature compensation devices on the balance or spring. Its non-magnetic properties were a bonus. Today hairsprings even in cheap watches are made of an alloy developed from Elinvar. Balance wheels in better watches are made of a new alloy, beryllium-bronze, which is extremely hard and almost entirely non-magnetic.

It is not 'human magnetism' but human reaction time that causes the biggest variables in using stop watches. A human timekeeper at an athletics meeting may have a reaction time of between a tenth and a third of a second. If he is 0.3 seconds late in starting his stop watch and 0.3 seconds late in stopping it, his timing will be accurate, however. Unfortunately there is not always this consistency.

Other errors have to be considered when timing races and record attempts. The first is the watch error. For races of a mile and less at athletic meetings, it is usual to use a timer reading to a tenth of a second. Such a watch can only show completed tenths of a second. It will therefore indicate the same time for runners about three feet apart in a hundred yeards race. A similar error can result from the usual practice of starting two timers simultaneously and timing the first runner with one and the next runner with the other.

In shorter races at important meetings, 1-100 second timers are used to eliminate watch errors, but human ones can, of course, remain. Over a period of time longer than it takes to run a mile, even expensive timers will have errors of fractions of a second in different positions, so time-of-day chronographs corrected for positional errors are more efficient.

A good human timekeeper has a reaction time of about

0.2 seconds which remains reasonably consistent. Waiting in line with the tape, he starts his timer at the flash of the starter's pistol and stops it when the runner's torso touches the tape. It has been found that the most usual cause of error in a human timekeeper is anticipation. If he watches the runners approach the tape he will record a slightly fast time. Experienced timekeepers fix their eyes on the far post when the runners are about five yards away.

Some watches have 'split seconds hands'. Two chronograph hands start together when the button is pressed but they can be stopped separately. If a timekeeper has to time another runner as well as the first one with a split-seconds timer, he will usually attribute too fast a time to the first runner because of anticipation.

In top class international events in most sports as well as in speed record attempts, timing equipment is often electric or electronic and the starting signal for the timer as well as the stopping signal is provided automatically. The starter's gun has a cable connected with the timing equipment to start it. A light beam in line with the tape, when broken by the first runner, stops the timing device.

There are many variations of this system depending on the sport and conditions. In ski slaloms, for example, a simple lever in front of the skier at the start provides the first timing signal. In swimming, touch pads at the end of the swimming bath give the times of each swimmer, making it possible to separate swimmers by fractions of an inch.

In horse and greyhound racing, where it is particularly important to separate the first four runners past the finishing post, the camera timer is used. It photographs the runners through a slit as they cross the line. The film in the camera is moved across the slit so that the camera does not provide an instantaneous picture of the finish like a normal camera. Instead, it photographs the part of each runner's body as it crosses the line. This accounts for the strange postures apparently adopted. The camera is linked with a timer and provides a photographic record of finishing times.

Cameras combined with timers are employed for very high speed record attempts, particularly in the air, when it is impossible to make the aircraft operate a physical device to start and stop the timing equipment. The aircraft is photographed by two linked timing cameras, one at the start and the other at the finish. In front of each camera is a datum post. From the times recorded on each film where the nose of the aircraft touches the

RIGHT: Clock operated by light and made by Patek Philippe, Geneva, Switzerland. The top contains a photo electric cell and can be turned to face the light. The photo cell drives a small motor which winds the clock. Four hours of light will run the clock for twenty-four hours GARRARD & CO., CROWN JEWELLERS, LONDON

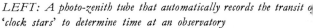

LEFT: *A photo-zenith tube that automatically records the transit of 'clock stars' to determine time at an observatory*

RIGHT: *Set-up for timing and televising a sports meeting so that viewers as well as spectators are given the times almost immediately. 1, synchronised starting pistol. 2-5, lights and photo-cells for stopping timer at finish. 7-8, electronic timers. 10, results board for spectators. 11-13, TV cameras covering meeting. 14, TV camera which photographs digital time recorder for superimposition on TV picture. 16, master quartz crystal clock*

post, the speed can be calculated.

The extensive television coverage given to Olympic sporting events has had its effect on timekeeping equipment because viewers like to know times as soon as a competitor crosses the line, especially when competitors are making separate runs against the clock, as in skiing. A system has been developed which shows the time on a television screen, below the picture. At the meeting a separate TV camera photographs a black screen, on the bottom of which the timers cause illuminated figures to appear. This is superimposed on the pictures from other TV cameras recording the race. There is also a link with a large timing dial at the meeting itself, so that the spectators are no less well informed than the television viewers.

Similar techniques are employed in measuring the trajectories of geodetic satellites, which give information about the Earth's mass, radius and local variations in gravity (previously measured by a change in rate of pendulum clocks) and also help in improving maps.

Tracking stations set up around the world record the heights and distances of these artificial satellites and the exact times of their passages. To do so, each station has

a theodolite, a recording chronograph, a quartz crystal clock, and a radio receiver. The quartz crystal clock controls the chronograph which photographs the theodolite reading and records the time to within about twenty milliseconds.

It is obviously extremely important for each tracking station to use the same time. After 1884, when the line of longitude through Greenwich was adopted as zero meridian by an international conference (only France and Ireland voting against the proposition), Greenwich Mean Time became the time scale for navigators in all parts of the world. GMT has proved insufficiently accurate in many of today's activities for various reasons. One is that, owing to irregularities in the rotation of the Earth, the zero meridian is constantly changing from one side to the other of the fixed line at Greenwich. In 1950, an international conference adopted what it called 'Universal Time' as the basis for civil timekeeping, navigating and surveying.

Universal Time is GMT corrected for movement of the Earth's axis and also for a nodding movement of the Earth during rotation, known as 'nutation'. It is still not absolutely uniform, as it is not practicable to make a

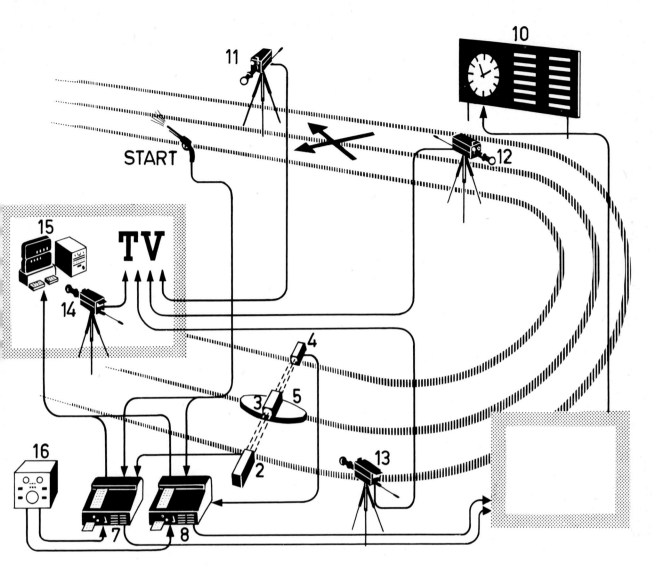

nown corrections. A time standard compensated for all nown variations including slowing down of the Earth called 'Uniform Time'.

Since 1st January, 1965, time has been based on a ew international unit of time. The second in time is ow defined by the caesium atomic clock instead of stronomical standards. The vibrating atom has proved be a better timekeeper than the stars. Applying accu- te corrections to time services is not simple, mainly ecause astronomical measurements have to be made efore the corrections are known and this may take a ear or more.

Universal Time is distributed by a network of twenty thirty time observatories which transmit time signals y radio. Their transmissions are checked by collaboration ith the Bureau International de l'Heure. The purpose f the radio receivers at the satellite tracking stations is compare the continuous time signals from one of the me observatories with the tracking stations' quartz ocks.

Although the atomic clock is now accepted as the most ccurate timekeeper, it is still vital to have more and ore accurate astronomical time to provide 'time mark-

ers'. The atomic clock provides the accurate timekeeper, but it still has to be 'set to time' by deciding what is the 'right time' by the stars.

Most observatories have a transit instrument to de- termine sidereal time. The transit instrument is a small telescope fixed so that it can swing only in a north- south direction. In the eyepiece is a vertical thread and a clock star is seen to move across this. As it does so, the astronomer operates a chronograph that records the transit of the star against the time shown by the obser- vatory clock. Routine checks are made on a number of stars to decide sidereal or star time which is converted to mean sidereal and ultimately mean solar time for daily use.

As the astronomer has to operate the chronograph, there are human errors which vary from one man to another. The latest astronomical instrument for time observations is the photo-zenith tube. It is a fixed vertical telescope which, after a button is pressed, automatically takes four photographs of a clock star by rotating the photographic plate 180° after each exposure. The result is four images of the star at the corners of a rectangle or parallelogram. The slope of the parallelogram indicates the human error in pressing the button, which can then be allowed for.

Another photographic plate in the photo-zenith tube makes a record of time by the observatory's quartz crystal clock, to compare it with the star transit.

Astronomers have to use time in another way. Owing to rotation of the Earth, a telescope will not remain pointed at a star, but gradually turns away. One of the earliest devices to swing a telescope backwards in relation to the movement of the Earth, and so 'follow' a star, was a cable attached to a heavy weight on a sand pit. As the weight sank, it pulled the telescope slowly round. The rate at which the telescope has to be moved is, of course, fifteen degrees an hour.

A mechanical clock with a conical pendulum driven by a weight was later devised to swing a telescope. The conical pendulum, the bob of which swings in a circle instead of to and fro, allows continuous, instead of intermittent movement. It became the centrifugal governor, as used on steam engines.

A governor employs the principle known as 'feed back'. It takes a sample of the movement of the telescope and applies a brake if the movement of the telescope is too rapid. It can only work when the motion is too great or too small. Its operation therefore causes oscillations or 'hunting'.

Because he had his telescope drives made so free and sensitive, a former Astronomer Royal, Sir George Airy, was plagued by his telescopes swinging backwards and forwards instead of remaining steadily on a star. The famous mathematician, Clerk Maxwell, solved the problem by suggesting that the friction in the mechanism should be increased to damp down the oscillations. This simple solution is common practice today.

The latest following drive for telescopes employs an ordinary electric motor driven from the electric mains, which runs slightly fast.

Impulses from the observatory clock 'monitor' the motor, keeping it down to the correct speed. The principle is the same as the free pendulum controlling a slave, described in the previous chapter.

Large observatories with quartz clock installations have the most accurate method. The high frequency of the clock is broken down to one that will drive an ordinary synchronous motor similar to that in ordinary domestic mains clocks. The clock signal is amplified enough for it to drive the motor swinging the telescope.

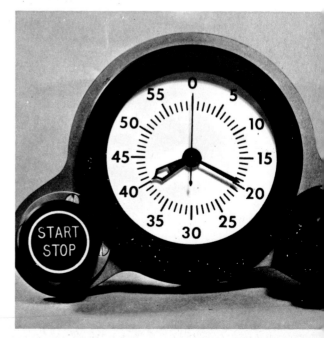

Time and timekeeping involve everybody. There is no escape from them, whether a man be a cowherd who is controlled by the rythm of milking time or an astronaut whose passage and life depend on the accuracy of quartz and atomic clocks. Many of the apparatuses of modern life include time bases, usually completely unsuspected by the users.

Index

Figures in italics indicate illustrations

Acknowledgements

The American Philosophical Society
Asprey's of Bond Street, London
Mr A. E. Ayres
Mr. Silvio Bedini, New York, USA
Biggs of Maidenhead
H. Blairman & Sons, London
Bowes Museum, Yorkshire
British Horological Institute, Nottingham Branch Antiquarian Group
British Museum
Mr. Sean Brown, Avoca, Eire
Caius College, Cambridge
Mr. T. P. Camerer Cuss, London
Mr. J. E. Coleman, Nashville, Tenn.
Collectors Pieces Exhibition, London
Ralph Cox, Lincoln
Christies, London
Deutsches Museum, Munich
Dresdener Zwinger, E. Germany
Mr. Ernest L. Edwardes, Sale
Garrard & Co., Crown Jewellers, London
Germanisches Nationalmuseum, Nuremberg
Hagans Clock Manor Museum, Colorado
Harris & Son, London

Her Majesty The Queen
Mr. Wallace Heaton, London
Dr. Lindsay, Astronomer Royal, Armagh, Northern Ireland
Mainfrankisches Museum
National Maritime Museum, Greenwich
National Museet, Copenhagen
National Physical Laboratory
The National Trust
H. M. Postmaster General
Mr. John Riddell, Armagh, Northern Ireland
James Robinson Inc., New York
Mr. T. R. Robinson, Bristol
Science Museum, London
The Smithsonian Institution, USA
Sotheby's, London
Jürg Stuker Gallery, Berne, Switzerland
Mr. Charles Terwilliger, New York
Ulster Museum, Northern Ireland
Usher Collection, City of Lincoln
Victoria & Albert Museum, London
Wilsdorf Collection at Rolex Watches, Geneva
Worshipful Company of Clockmakers, London
Wuppertaler Uhrenmuseum, W. Germany

Fig. 2.

Fig. 3.